MODERN CHINESE MILITARY AIRCRAFT
1990–Present

MODERN CHINESE MILITARY AIRCRAFT
1990–Present

RYAN CUNNINGHAM

First published in 2024

Copyright © 2024 Amber Books Ltd

All rights reserved. No part of this publication may be reproduced, stored in a retrieval system, or transmitted in any form or by any means, electronic, mechanical, photocopying, recording, or otherwise, without prior written permission of the copyright holder.

Published by Amber Books Ltd
United House
London N7 9DP
United Kingdom
www.amberbooks.co.uk
Facebook: amberbooks
YouTube: amberbooksltd
Instagram: amberbooksltd
X(Twitter): @amberbooks

ISBN: 978-1-83886-349-4

Editor: Michael Spilling
Designer: Mark Batley
Picture research: Terry Forshaw
Additional text: Edward Ward

Printed in China

Contents

Introduction	6
Fighters & Interceptors	8
Bombers & Attack Aircraft	44
Transports	54
Special Mission Aircraft	72
Helicopters	96
Unmanned Aerial Vehicles	106
Trainers	116
INDEX	124
PICTURE CREDITS	128

Introduction

To a significant degree, the current trajectory of the People's Liberation Army Air Force (PLAAF) – the flying branch of the armed forces of the People's Republic of China – has been influenced by major political developments that occurred in the 1980s.

Many of the aircraft types included in this book, but especially those that currently play the most important role within the structure of the PLAAF, had their fates determined in this period, which saw upheavals not only for the Chinese military but for the country as a whole.

As of the late 1980s, China maintained a good relationship with various Western aircraft and arms manufacturers and was hopeful that the introduction of new types incorporating advanced technologies developed in Europe and the United States would precipitate an overhaul of the PLAAF and its capabilities. In this way, the air arm would break away from the traditionally Soviet-era doctrine and hardware that had been inherited from the era of Chairman Mao's Cultural Revolution, and emerge as a truly modern air force, with more Western-style equipment and tactics.

The bloody events in Tiananmen Square in 1989 brought these aspirations to a swift end. The hopes of cooperation with Western manufacturers were quickly dashed and, instead, Beijing turned to Moscow to meet its immediate demands for more capable combat aircraft and related equipment. At the same time, efforts to domestically develop aircraft – as well as advanced weapons and avionics – were stepped up in China.

A PLAAF Xi'an Y-20 transport is seen here at Sheremetyevo International Airport, Russia, during a diplomatic visit, June 2020.

INTRODUCTION

A Shenyang J-16 fighter jet performs aerial manoeuvres during Airshow China 2022, in Zhuhai, Guangdong Province, China.

The arrival of the Sukhoi Su-27 'Flanker' from Russia was a highly important step, finally providing the PLAAF with what, in Western terms at least, was a true fourth-generation fighter. Additional and further advanced Sukhoi designs would follow in the 1990s and 2000s, as China increasingly embraced a concept of warfare that was closer to Western models and heavily influenced by the lessons of the 1991 Gulf War.

Indigenous output

From this point onwards, the PLAAF placed an increasing emphasis on high-tech warfare, including improved situational awareness and command-and-control functions. While China's military leaders may have understood the challenges of this new doctrine, the combat aircraft that were being supplied by Russia often failed to fit into this concept of thinking. The result was a further push to enhance China's indigenous aerospace output, with the fourth-generation Chengdu J-10, for example, being followed by the Chengdu J-20 that offers fifth-generation technologies: stealth features, advanced radar and electro-optical sensors, a high level of performance and agility, and more.

The J-20 may be a flagship project of China's aerospace industries and a key part of the PLAAF's modernization, but it is only one element. In the meantime, China has been busily further developing the 'Flanker' airframe to produce a range of successively more capable versions, with a growing proportion of domestic components, including engines and weapons. The J-10, too, has been further optimized, creating a more capable and versatile fighter with true multirole capabilities.

These fighters are mentioned here primarily to reflect the pace of development of the PLAAF since Tiananmen Square, and the unique approach taken to establishing a modern air arm. As this book should make clear, however, fighters are just one element of a modern air force, with bombers, electronic warfare and reconnaissance, transport and aerial refuelling tankers, helicopters, drones and trainers being just as important.

Overall, after addressing multiple challenges, the prospects for the future of the PLAAF looks brighter than ever.

FIGHTERS & INTERCEPTORS

The cutting edge of the PLAAF is provided by its fighters. The pace of modernization of the service is reflected in the fighter force. The J-7 and J-8, designs that date back to the 1950s and 1960s respectively, are on the verge of disappearing entirely. The importance of Russian-supplied Su-27s and Su-30s is starting to diminish, in favour of more advanced Chinese 'Flanker' derivatives – chiefly the J-16 – as well as the fully indigenous fourth-generation J-10 and fifth-generation J-20.

- Chengdu J-7
- Shenyang J-8
- Chengdu J-10
- Shenyang J-11 and J11A
- Shenyang J-11B
- Shanyang J-16
- Chengdu J-20
- Sukhoi Su-27
- Sukhoi Su-30
- Sukhoi Su-35

Chengdu J-20 stealth fighter jets fly in formation during Airshow China 2022, in Zhuhai, Guangdong Province, China.

FIGHTERS & INTERCEPTORS

Chengdu J-7

For many years, the backbone of the People's Liberation Army Air Force (PLAAF) fighter fleet was provided by the J-7, a locally produced version of the ubiquitous Soviet-designed Mikoyan-Gurevich MiG-21.

Today, more advanced versions of the J-7 remain in PLAAF service albeit in very limited numbers, with reequipment of the few remaining units continuing apace.

Beijing selected the MiG-21 as its next fighter to follow on from the Shenyang J-6, a licence-built version of the MiG-19. However, this new effort would be hampered by the deteriorating relationship between China and the Soviet Union. Despite the political obstacles, a licence agreement covering Chinese production of the MiG-21F-13 version, as well as its R-11F-300 turbojet engine, was agreed in 1961.

Plans called for Moscow to deliver three MiG-21F-13 'pattern' aircraft as well as 20 more aircraft in kit form for assembly in China. Unfortunately, politics got in the way, and the Soviets suspended the delivery of these items. Instead, Shenyang began to reverse engineer the MiG-21 from 1962 onwards. This was not an easy process, and construction of a prototype J-7, based on the fairly primitive MiG-21F-13, would not begin until 1964. The R-11F-300 engine, meanwhile, was reverse-engineered as the WP-7.

First flight

The first 'Chinese-built' MiG-21 took to the air in January 1966, but this was likely one of the Soviet-supplied kits, and the programme continued to experience difficulties. Although Beijing approved production in June 1967, the aircraft and engine were far from ready. The PLAAF was left disappointed, and production had to be stopped in 1970.

Another effort to locally manufacture the MiG-21 was then launched by Chengdu, which had meanwhile assumed responsibility for J-7 production. Chengdu made improvements to the design, and flight testing of the new prototype began in June 1969. Like the previous Shenyang model, the first of the Chengdu variants also failed to enter quantity production or frontline service.

It was not until the J-7I (alternatively known as the J-7A) first flown in April 1970 that China finally had a fully operational version of the MiG-21 that was also suitable for large-scale manufacturing. However, the programme experienced delays, and it was only in June 1975 that this aircraft was formally approved for service.

Chengdu J-7
Weight (maximum take-off): 7540kg (16,623lb)
Dimensions: Length: 14.88m (48ft 10in), Wingspan 8.32m (27ft 4in), Height 4.11m (13ft 6in)
Powerplant: One Liyang Wopen-13F afterburning turbojet, 44.1kN (9,900lbf) thrust dry
Maximum speed: 2200km/h (1,400mph, 1,200kn)
Range: 850km (530 mi, 460 nmi)
Ceiling: 17,500m (57,400ft)
Crew: 1
Armament: Two 30mm (1.18in) Type 30-1 cannon, 60 rounds per gun; five hardpoints: four underwing, up to 500kg (1100lb) each, one centerline under-fuselage 2000kg (4,400lb) maximum; 55mm rocket pod (12 rounds), 90mm rocket pod (7 rounds)

Chengdu J-7L
This PLAAF J-7, serial number 21002, was seen at Dalian Zhoushuizi International Airport, China, in 2016.

FIGHTERS & INTERCEPTORS

A Chengdu J-7FS, serial number 21864 'Red', 15th Fighter Division, 44th Air Regiment, PLAAF, flying from Yongning Air Base, 2004.

Even then, it was a strictly limited day fighter, with technology that was by then thoroughly obsolescent. The build quality of the J-7I was also disappointing, and this helped contribute to a production run of only 188 aircraft, the last of which was completed in 1981.

Extensive changes

More thorough changes were then embodied in the J-7II (also known as the J-7A), another Chengdu product, work on which had been launched by 1974. Externally, the J-7II could be differentiated by its redesigned cockpit canopy, below which was a new ejection seat, while the powerplant was the improved WP-7B and the avionics were enhanced. Another distinguishing feature was the revised tailfin, with a container for the brake chute now added at its root.

After its maiden flight in December 1978, the J-7II was approved for service in September 1979. The demand for the new fighter was such that a new production line was opened by Guizhou. Between them, Chengdu and Guizhou produced around 475 J-7IIs up until 1986. For the PLAAF, the J-7II was numerically important but the time it had taken to bring it into service meant that, once again, it was technologically outdated by the time it was introduced.

Attempted improvements

Some efforts were made to improve the J-7II. However, most of these were aimed at export customers. The J-7IIA of 1982 added Western avionics, as well as a Type 226 radar, while the J-7IIH came as standard with four underwing weapons pylons and could use the PL-8 air-to-air missile (AAM).

By 1977–78, Chengdu had been requested to start work on a further improved J-7 variant, namely the J-7III (or J-7C). This was inspired by the Soviet MiG-21MF and, as such, was to incorporate all-weather and day and night capabilities. Work was undertaken jointly by Chengdu and Guizhou using a number of Egyptian-supplied MiG-21MFs, which began to arrive in China in 1979.

The J-7III first flew in April 1984 and brought with it a host of new features, including a JL-7 air-intercept radar, a head-up display and countermeasures dispensers. It was also fitted with a more powerful WP-13 engine. However, the 'third-generation' J-7 did not meet

11

PLAAF expectations, and only a limited production run followed, with deliveries from December 1989.

An effort to further enhance the J-7III resulted in the J-7IIIA, launched in 1988, with a more reliable WP-13FI engine and upgraded avionics. This entered production as the J-7D, identified by the prominent countermeasures dispensers on each side of the tailfin. This was first flown in August 1991, but only 32 were completed.

J-7E

After the failure of the J-7III/J-7C, Chengdu went back to the drawing board with a new design that was based on the airframe of the original J-7II. The aim was to improve agility, as well as add more fuel and more advanced armament, including PL-8 AAMs.

Development began in 1987, resulting in the J-7E, and the major change was a redesigned 'double-delta' wing planform. Combined with a more powerful WP-13F engine, agility was much improved.

Revised avionics included a Type 226 radar and a cockpit with 'hands-on throttle and stick' (HOTAS) controls. First flown in May 1990, 263 J-7Es were delivered up until 2001, including land-based naval (J-7EH) and aerobatic (J-7EB) versions.

J-7G

Inspired by the success of the F-7MG and F-7PG versions of the J-7E, which were produced for export, Chengdu embarked on a new PLAAF version known as the J-7G. Avionics were further improved, including a KLJ-6E pulse-Doppler radar, while a one-piece windshield provided the pilot with much better visibility. First flown in June 2002, a reported 128 examples were built up until 2009. Thereafter, some of the PLAAF's J-7Es were also modified with the J-7G's systems, receiving the new designation J-7L.

Shenyang J-8

Alongside the MiG-21-derived J-7, successive versions of the significantly larger Shenyang J-8 – which received the Western reporting name 'Finback' – served the PLAAF for many years, although the type is now very much in the twilight of its career, being flown by only a handful of units.

By 1964, work on a successor to the J-7 had been launched at the Chinese Academy of Engineering, after which Shenyang began to examine two different potential development paths. One was an all-new single-engine fighter powered by a new turbofan engine, known as the J-9. Somewhat less ambitious was a further development of the basic J-7 configuration with two engines and optimized for high-altitude interception – this was the J-8.

Delayed production

In the event, Shenyang opted for the more conservative J-8, essentially an enlarged J-7, with large delta wings, a nose intake containing a Type 204 fire-control radar and a wider fuselage containing a pair of WP-7A turbojets. The first pair of J-8 prototypes were completed in July 1968, with first flight recorded in July 1969. However, amid the turmoil of the Cultural Revolution, further development was painfully slow. It was only once the political situation had stabilized that work properly resumed, with official certification of the design in March 1980.

J-8I/A

With so much time having passed, the J-8 was now entirely outdated, so Shenyang began work on an improved version: the J-8I (alternatively known as the J-8A). Improvements introduced by the J-8I or J-8A included new avionics, among them a Type 204 radar, while a new HTY-2 ejection seat was installed below a revised cockpit canopy. A new twin-barrel Type 23-III cannon was fitted, with missile armament comprising up to four PL-2B or PL-5B air-to-air missiles (AAMs).

The first prototype of the J-8I was completed in May 1980, and the flight test programme was finished by November 1985. The J-8I still did not meet the PLAAF's requirements, however, so production was cut short, ending in 1987.

J-8II/B

A much more thorough redesign of the basic aircraft then produced the J-8II (or J-8B), which emerged from a requirement issued in September 1980, with work beginning in 1982. The J-8II looked considerably different,

FIGHTERS & INTERCEPTORS

Shenyang J-8F
This J-8F, serial number 72200, was seen at Changchun Dafangshen Airport in October 2019. The J-8F was a development of the J-8C, but equipped with JL-10 (Type 1473) radar and PL-11 medium-range semi-active radar homing (SARH) air-to-air missile (AAM).

Shenyang JZ-8F
The JZ-8F was a reconnaissance version of the J-8F with the Type 23-III cannon replaced by an internal camera.

retaining much of the existing rear fuselage but adding a forward end that featured two lateral engine air intakes and a large radome. A huge new tailfin was also fitted.

The first prototype J-8II took to the air in June 1984, and testing continued until 1988. However, the PLAAF was still unconvinced about the fighter's capabilities and sought to integrate Western avionics in conjunction with the US firm Grumman under the Peace Pearl programme.

Despite J-8IIs being modified and tested in the United States, for political reasons this effort came to an end in 1989. However, a production run of around 54 'standard' J-8IIs followed from 1992 to 1995.

The next development was the J-8IIA, first flown in November 1989, otherwise known as J-8II Batch 02. This became the definitive J-8B, and it featured a strengthened airframe that allowed it to carry heavier payloads.

Refuelling capability
Around the same time, work was also underway on the J-8IIB (also known as the J-8D), which added an inflight refuelling capability and first flew in November 1990. It was primarily developed for land-based naval use. Both the J-8IIA and J-8IIB lacked a true beyond-visual-range engagement capability, which was planned to be addressed in the J-8III (or J-8C). This was to bring a true multirole capability, although it was abandoned after a handful of prototypes – China instead decided

---

Shenyang J-8F
Weight (maximum take-off): 15,288kg (33,704lb)
Dimensions: Length: 21.39m (70ft 2in), Wingspan 9.34m (30ft 8in), Height 5.41m (17ft 9in)
Powerplant: Two Guizhou WP-13B afterburning turbojet engines, 47.1kN (10,580lbf) thrust each dry, 68.6kN (15,430lbf) with afterburner
Maximum speed: Mach 1.8
Range: 1000km (620 mi, 540 nmi) with drop tanks
Ceiling: 18,000m (59,000ft)
Crew: 1
Armament: One 23mm (0.9in) Type 23-III cannon; one centreline and six under-wing hardpoints with a capacity of three drop tanks; two PL-11 missiles SARH AAM

FIGHTERS & INTERCEPTORS

A Shenyang J-8 fighter lands at the 24th Air Division base, Yangcun, located around 100 kilometers (62 miles) southeast of Beijing, July 2002.

to purchase Sukhoi Su-27s from the Soviet Union.

Shenyang did not abandon the J-8 at this point and instead looked at other ways of improving it. After around 80 of the J-8IIA and J-8IIB (J-8B and J-8D) had been produced in the second half of the 1990s, some survivors were retrofitted with a new Type 1471 radar that provided the ability to use the medium-range PL-11 AAM with semi-active radar homing. In the process, the aircraft were redesignated as the J-8BH or J-8DH, and a small batch of new-production J-8H fighters was also completed starting in 2001 – around 24 in all.

Production of the J-8H was quickly superseded by the J-8F, development of which began in 1997. First flown in 2000, the J-8F includes a new Type 1492 pulse-Doppler radar, which is compatible with the PL-12 AAM, an advanced weapon with active radar homing, providing a 'fire and forget' capability. The revised cockpit features digital displays and a head-up display, while the powerplant is made up of two WP-13BII engines. As well as production of around 56 J-8Fs from 2003–08, a number of existing J-8Ds were brought up to the same standard as the J-8DF.

J-8 reconnaissance versions
The first reconnaissance 'Finbacks' were produced via conversion of the early J-8I version in the mid-1980s. This produced the JZ-8, which was fitted with a large pod under its fuselage containing several cameras.

The JZ-8 remained in PLAAF service until the early 2000s, when it was replaced by the JZ-8F, a reconnaissance development of the J-8F. Optimized for tactical reconnaissance, the JZ-8F has a semi-recessed camera pack below the cockpit where the cannon would normally be found. Various different configurations have been noted, suggesting that different cameras can be installed. This aircraft reportedly entered service in 2006 with a limited production run only.

Finally, there is also a suppression of enemy air defences (SEAD) version, known as the J-8G, which first flew in June 2001. This can be armed with a pair of YJ-91/Kh-31P anti-radiation missiles to target hostile ground-based air defence systems, which are identified using a hemispherical electronic support measures (ESM) antenna below the forward fuselage.

FIGHTERS & INTERCEPTORS

Chengdu J-10

The most numerous fully indigenous fighter in PLAAF use, the J-10 is nothing less than a milestone in China's military aviation, as the country's first true fourth-generation multirole fighter to enter production and service.

A PLAAF Chengdu J-10A jet fighter lands at Dyagilevo Air Base, Russia, during the Aviadarts 2019 competition.

After many false starts, the J-10 has demonstrated that China is capable of successfully developing a homegrown combat aircraft. The aircraft is known in China by the popular name 'Vigorous Dragon', while the Western reporting name 'Firebird' has also been attributed to it.

Before the dragon

China began to lay the foundations for the J-10 in the early 1980s when it formalized a requirement for a single-engine multirole type that would be able to replace not only the J-7 in the air defence role but also the Nanchang Q-5 'Fantan' attack aircraft. However, development took some time to advance, primarily due to the lack of a suitable engine. In terms of its configuration, Chengdu selected a tailless delta configuration with canard foreplanes and a chin-mounted engine intake. This was the result of earlier design studies, including for the J-9, another Chengdu fighter project that had been abandoned in 1980. When development of the J-10 was formally launched in 1984, the design was still known as the J-9VI or J-9B.

As well as the J-9, it seems likely that there was (at least) some design influence from Israel in the creation of the Vigorous Dragon. Much has been made of the conceptual similarities between the J-10 and the Israel Aircraft Industries (IAI) Lavi fighter, although the two aircraft are of different size, the Chinese fighter being notably bigger and heavier.

Whatever the relationship that exists between the J-10 and the Lavi, it's clear that there was contact between IAI and Chengdu around the time that

FIGHTERS & INTERCEPTORS

the Chinese jet was being developed. Reportedly, the main areas of exchange involved development of fly-by-wire (FBW) controls and integration of modern flight control systems.

Delays to the programme also resulted from the Chinese aerospace industry focusing on the J-8II, which was consuming considerable funds. At the same time, changes were being made to the J-10 design, and development did not really start to pick up pace until the early 1990s.

Prototype and flight testing

A full-size wooden mock-up of the J-10 was completed in 1991, with hopes of having a prototype in the air by 1996. However, problems in the development of the planned WP-15 (and later WS-10) engine seem to have almost led to the cancellation of the entire project. The mock-up featured a Chinese engine, but in the absence of this hardware, Chengdu then opted for the Russian-made AL-31FN turbofan, which necessitated a partial redesign – as well as extensive negotiations with Moscow. It was this engine that powered the first prototype J-10, which was completed in June 1997 and performed its maiden flight on 23 March 1998. Flight testing then apparently proceeded fairly smoothly and was completed by the end of 2003, by which time series production had already been launched. The new fighter was ready for service with the PLAAF in June 2004.

J-10A, J-10AH and J-10ASH

Three batches of the initial-production J-10 were swiftly followed by the J-10A with various minor avionics improvements, including the more capable Type 1473G fire-control radar and a revised cockpit. Original J-10s were later modified to the same standards. A derivative of the J-10A is the J-10AH for land-based naval service. There is also a tandem-seat trainer version of the J-10A, designated J-10AS, which features a prominent single canopy and a

The afterburner of the Chengdu J-10A's Saturn AL-31FN turbofan engine is obvious in this photograph. The J-10A can reach a maximum speed of Mach 2.1 (2593.08m/h).

FIGHTERS & INTERCEPTORS

Chengdu J-10B
Serial number 1035 is understood to be the fifth prototype J-10B and was retained by Chengdu for trials work. While the J-10B introduced a new X-band passive electronically-scanned array radar, this is replaced on the definitive J-10C by an active electronically scanned array.

Chengdu J-10B
A J-10B, serial number 10537, of the PLAAF's 5th Regiment, 2nd Division, based at Guilin, China.

large dorsal spine to accommodate the electronics displaced by the rear cockpit. The two-seater is also fully combat-capable. It was first flown in 2003 and entered service in 2005–06. In naval use, the trainer version is the J-10ASH.

The J-10's advanced cockpit is equipped with a wide-angle head-up display (HUD), two monochrome multifunctional displays (MFDs) and one colour MFD. The pilot is provided with a helmet-mounted sight and 'hands-on throttle and stick' (HOTAS) controls. As well as the Type 1473 pulse-Doppler fire-control radar, other avionics items include GPS/inertial navigation system, air data computer, radar warning receiver, Type 634 digital quadruplex FBW controls, digital fuel management system, mission management system and an ARINC 429 data bus for stores management.

The J-10 was introduced to service with a relatively basic air-to-air armament based around the short-range PL-8 infrared-guided and the medium-range PL-11 semi-active radar-guided air-to-air missiles (AAMs). The aircraft has progressively received new weapons and sensor pods, including medium-range PL-12 active-radar-guided AAMs. To increase missile carriage capacity, a new twin-rail launch pylon was also introduced for the PL-12. More recently, the PL-8 and PL-12 have begun to be superseded by the new-generation PL-10 and PL-15 respectively.

Chengdu J-10B
Weight (maximum take-off): 20,500kg (45,195lb)
Dimensions: Length 16.03m (52ft 7in), Wingspan 9.25m (30ft 4in), Height 5.43m (17ft 10in)
Powerplant: One Saturn AL-31FN M1 turbofan engine rated at 79.43kN (17,860lb) of thrust with afterburning
Maximum speed: Mach 2.1
Range: 2250km (1400 miles)
Ceiling: 17,000m (56,000ft)
Crew: 1
Armament: One 23mm (0.9in) twin-barrel GSh-23 cannon plus a maximum of 6800kg (15,400lb) of disposable stores carried on 11 hardpoints

FIGHTERS & INTERCEPTORS

Typical armament configurations
For offensive missions, a typical weapons load includes LS-500J precision-guided bombs used in conjunction with a forward-looking infrared/laser targeting pod, another item that was added later. Two of the 500kg (1102lb) LS-500Js or the newer GB1/TG500 bombs can be carried alongside a K/JDC01A targeting pod and a K/RKL700A electronic countermeasures (ECM) pod.

For suppression of enemy air defences (SEAD), the normal armament is a pair of YJ-91 anti-radiation missiles, a single CM802AKG guidance pod and a K/RKL700A ECM pod. Reportedly, more than 224 single-seat J-10As and around 48 two-seat J-10AS aircraft were completed, with production taking place between 2002 and 2014.

J-10B
Unveiled in late 2008, the J-10B is a much-improved development of the fighter characterized by its fixed diverter-less supersonic inlet (DSI), a feature that reduces structural weight and improves radar cross-section. Meanwhile, a re-profiled radome houses an X-band passive electronically scanned array (PESA) radar said to be able to track 10 targets and engage four of them simultaneously. Other new features include an infrared search and track sensor in front of the cockpit, three colour MFDs in the cockpit and a holographic wide-angle HUD. While the first J-10Bs retained the AL-31FN, the fifth prototype appeared with the indigenous WS-10B engine in 2011, although the subsequent production batch then reverted to the Russian powerplant, presumably due to ongoing problems with the Chinese engine, although it is notable that the Chinese engine had begun to be installed in all production J-11 and J-16 fighters some years before it appeared in series-built J-10s. A total of around 56 J-10Bs were completed.

Ground crew prepare a J-10 August 1st demonstration team fighter for flight at Airshow China 2014 in Zhuhai, Guangdong Province, China.

FIGHTERS & INTERCEPTORS

Chengdu J-10C

This J-10C, coded 74826, was seen at Zhuhai in November 2022, in low-viz markings. It carries drop tanks on the centreline and inboard wing pylons, with PL-15 missiles on the wing pylons and empty intake pylons, as well as countermeasure dispenser units on the rear fuselage.

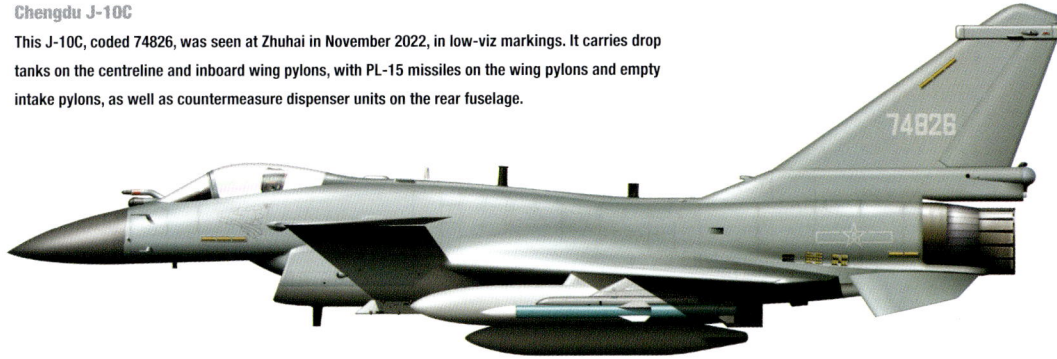

AUGUST 1 DEMONSTRATION TEAM

Minor modifications to the single-seater and two-seater versions of the J-10A produced the J-10AY and J-10SY sub-variants that were operated by the PLAAF's aerial demonstration team, known as 'August 1' (or Ba Yi, to give its Chinese name). In a surprise move, a further modified aircraft for the same demonstration team then appeared in mid-2022. This features a very prominent enlarged fuselage spine, leading to early suggestions it may have been a dedicated SEAD model, tentatively dubbed J-10D. In fact, the 'big spine' J-10 is thought to be designated J-10CY and is a new version of the J-10C variant intended specifically for service with the August 1 team.

Chengdu J-10CY

A J-10CY flown by the August 1st Demonstration Team, PLAAF.

Chengdu J-10C

Weight (maximum take-off): 20,500kg (45,195lb)
Dimensions: Length 16.9m (55ft 5in), Wingspan 9.8m (32ft 2in), Height 5.7m (18ft 8in)
Powerplant: One WS-10B afterburning turbofan engines, 89.17kN (20,050lbf) thrust dry, 144kN (32,000lbf) with afterburner
Maximum speed: Mach 1.8
Range: 2250km (1400 miles)
Ceiling: 18,000m (59,000ft)
Crew: 1
Armament: One 23mm (0.9in) twin-barrel GSh-23 cannon plus a maximum of 6800kg (15,400lb) of disposable stores carried on 11 hardpoints, including PL-15 air-to-air missiles

J-10C

In 2016, the J-10B was superseded by the J-10C, which introduced the definitive radar, incorporating an active electronically scanned array (AESA). Since around 2019, the WS-10 engine has been fitted as standard in the J-10C, while one of the J-10B aircraft has also been tested with a thrust-vectoring version of the same engine, although it is unclear if this is intended for future production versions too. It may well be the case that the thrust-vectoring J-10B instead primarily serves as an engine testbed for the J-20 fifth-generation fighter.

FIGHTERS & INTERCEPTORS

Shenyang J-11 and J-11A

After turning to the Soviet Union to fulfil its immediate fourth-generation fighter needs with the Sukhoi Su-27 'Flanker', China also secured a deal for the licence production of those same jets, with the local work to be undertaken by Shenyang.

The terms of this deal were included in Beijing's second Su-27 contract, dated May 1995, which also covered 16 single-seat Su-27SKs and eight two-seat Su-27UBKs. When the licence production deal was finally signed in December 1995, it covered the Chinese manufacture of 200 Su-27SKs. They would be supplied to China in kit form by the Komsomolsk-on-Amur Aircraft Production Association (KNAAPO) plant in the Russian Far East, together with their Lyulka (later NPO Lyulka/Saturn) AL-31F turbofan engines and various items of weaponry.

It seems that the deal also included the introduction of progressively more Chinese-furnished components, although a minimum of 30 per cent Russian content was stipulated. The Shenyang-produced Su-27SK is known as the J-11 but is otherwise similar to the Russian product.

Maiden flight and origins
Reportedly, the first two locally assembled Su-27SKs completed their maiden flights in December 1998. The two aircraft appear to have been delivered to the PLAAF in September 1999. It is unclear exactly how many kit-form Su-27SKs were completed (as J-11s) by Shenyang. It seems possible that only around 40 of these original J-11s were built before production switched to an improved version known as the J-11A.

The origins of the J-11A appear to lie in disputes waged between China and Russia as to the terms of the licence manufacturing deal. In particular, it seems the PLAAF was disappointed with the performance of the N001 radar, but Russia initially refused to upgrade it.

This meant the J-11 (like the Su-27SK) remained primarily an air defence asset, lacking the true

Shenyang J-11A
Weight (maximum take-off): 33,000kg (72,753lb)
Dimensions: Length: 21.9m (69ft 6in) without probe, Wingspan 14.7m (48ft 3in), Height 5.7m (18ft 9in)
Powerplant: Two AL-31F series 3 turbofans, each rated at 122.5kN (27,558lb) with afterburning
Maximum speed: 2500km/h (1600mph) at altitude
Range: 3530km (2190 miles)
Ceiling: 19,000m (62,336ft)
Crew: 1
Armament: One GSh-301 30mm (1.2in) cannon, plus disposable stores carried on 10 hardpoints

Shenyang J-11A
This aircraft was displayed in this special scheme as part of the celebrations around the 60th anniversary of the PLAAF, held at Beijing Shahezhen Airbase in November 2009. The camouflage is a variation of the darker grey and it has anti-collision strips on the nose, intakes and fins. It is thought to be from the 4th Regiment of the 2nd Air Division, based at Liuzhou.

multirole capability that the Chinese military had long desired. Whatever the details, in late 2000, Shenyang announced that not all the 200 Su-27s covered by the licencing deal would necessarily have to be assembled from kits, suggesting that there was by now an impetus to develop an improved Chinese version of the J-11, likely with multirole capability.

Production and refinements

Reportedly, the J-11A began its flight test programme in December 1999 and entered production by 2002 (if not earlier). By now, Russia had also relented on the radar dispute, supplying the improved N001VE system. Also included was a modernized cockpit featuring two small colour multifunctional displays (MFDs). The new radar also allowed the use of the Russian-made R-77 (AA-12 'Adder') active-radar-guided air-to-air missile (AAM).

Further improvements were introduced as J-11A production continued. These included changes to the cockpit, adding a new liquid-crystal MFD, which was also installed

retroactively on older jets. Some J-11As have also received a GPS display in the cockpit. Meanwhile, both J-11s and J-11As have been seen fitted with a new UV-band missile approach warning system (MAWS) with antennas behind the cockpit and on the sides of the tailfins.

Uncertain total

Once again, it remains unclear exactly how many J-11As were produced,

A J-11A fighter takes off from a PLAAF air base during training in Zhejiang province, east China, August 2021.

although reliable sources suggest that perhaps around 65 examples were completed before production was discontinued in 2006. After this point, the Shenyang facility switched over to the manufacture of the more capable J-11B, with much more indigenous content. This aircraft also differed in

FIGHTERS & INTERCEPTORS

being built by China without any (known) licencing agreement.

Some sources put the total number of J-11 and J-11A aircraft completed at 104 or 105. Other sources suggest that not all of these were actually completed and handed over to the PLAAF. Regardless, at least some of the surviving J-11s were gradually upgraded to J-11A standard during their service lives.

J-11 vs Su-27SK

In terms of distinguishing a Chinese-assembled J-11 from a Su-27SK, this is essentially impossible without reference to the construction number. However, the subsequent J-11A does present some differences, including the antennas for the radar warning receivers (RWR). Most obviously, the small fairing on top of the tailfin is deleted on the J-11A. Bearing in mind their age, the

A twin-engined Shenyang J-11 fighter plane coming in to land at Jiaxing, China, February 2021.

J-11 and J-11A are the least capable 'Flanker' versions in service with the PLAAF, and they are notably limited by their older Russian air-to-air armament, in contrast to the more modern weapons available to the J-11B, let alone to the multirole-capable J-16.

Shenyang J-11A
This J-11A, 'Yellow 10182', is believed to be from the 7th Division's 19th Regiment, based at Zhangjiakou. It is wearing special red stripe markings on the IR seeker, tail stinger and wing tip rails and a double stripe behind the canopy, as special markings for the 70th China Victory Day parade in August 2015. The intake serial number is 0317 and the aircraft has the usual mix of semi-active radar homing R-27 (AA-10 Alamo-A) and infra-red homing R-73 (AA-11 Archer) air-to-air missiles beneath the wings.

FIGHTERS & INTERCEPTORS

Shenyang J-11B

The J-11B series, which has the Western reporting name 'Flanker-L', represents the full Chinese indigenization of the original Soviet-era Sukhoi Su-27 design.

Shenyang J-11B

This Shenyang J-11B, coded 70005, is thought to be from the 89th Brigade, Northern Theatre Command, based at Pulandian. The B version includes more Chinese-produced features, such as the WS-10 engines, the characteristic, redesigned wing tip pylons and various sensor changes around the airframe. It is painted in the darker, bluer 'gunship' scheme with solid black radome and has a PL-15 extended-range, active-radar homing air-to-air missile under its wings.

Shenyang J-11B
Weight (maximum take-off): 33,000kg (72,753lb)
Dimensions: Length: 21.9m (69ft 6in),
Wingspan 14.7m (48ft 3in), Height 5.92m (19ft 5in)
Powerplant: Two Shenyang WS-10A 'Taihang' afterburning turbofans, 132kN (30,000lbf) thrust each (Block 02)
Maximum speed: Mach 2.35 (2500km/h, 1553mph)
Range: 3530km (2190 mi, 1,910 nmi)
Ceiling: 19,000m (62,000ft)
Crew: 1
Armament: One 30mm (1.18in) Gryazev-Shipunov GSh-30-1 cannon with 150 rounds; 10 hardpoints: two under fuselage, two under air ducts, four under wings, four on wingtips, with provisions to carry PL-12 and PL-15 air-to-air missiles

Whereas the J-11 and J-11A involved licence production of the Su-27 followed by modest improvements and in-service upgrades, with the J-11B, the PLAAF finally achieved its ambition of fielding a more capable fourth generation 'Flanker' and one over which it had full control.

The J-11B project appears to have been launched in 2002. After testing some systems on a pair of modified J-11s, the first true J-11B prototype reportedly took to the air in June 2004. Production likely began sometime in 2006, although there seem to have been delays relating to both the new flight control system and the domestically produced WS-10 Taihang engine. Development of the WS-10 actually seems to have predated the launch of the J-11B programme, with a J-11 reported to have flown with one of its AL-31F engines replaced by the Chinese powerplant in 2001 or 2002.

Engine issues

As it was, the first batch of J-11Bs was grounded due to problems with their WS-10s, which were ultimately re-engined with Russian-made AL-31Fs. By 2009, engine issues appear to have been resolved and subsequent J-11Bs were powered by the WS-10A as standard. Production of the aircraft seems to have been completed in 2018, however, with Shenyang thereafter focusing on the two-seat multirole J-16.

The J-11B not only provided the PLAAF with a 'Flanker' with domestically produced engines but also Chinese avionics, including a Type 1493 multi-mode pulse-Doppler radar and fire-control system. As well as locally developed radar, the J-11B is reportedly equipped with an indigenous electro-optical sighting system made up of an infrared search and track (IRST) sensor and a new helmet-mounted sight.

The J-11B also employs a Chinese-developed modern cockpit with digital displays, including five colour multifunction displays (MFDs) and a new wide-angle holographic head-up display (HUD).

Additional changes

Other changes found on the J-11B are thought to include a new three-axis digital flight-control system and revised avionics, apparently resulting in almost the complete replacement of the previous Russian equipment.

There are other new features, too, increasing the Chinese content of the

FIGHTERS & INTERCEPTORS

A J-11BS is put through its paces. The J-11BS includes the domestically-produced Taihang engine (the Shenyang WS-10), an upgrade on earlier J-11 models.

aircraft. Less obvious, perhaps, is the widespread use of composite materials in the aircraft's construction, which results in reduced structural weight, in turn allowing heavier payloads to be carried. The previous Russian electronic countermeasures suite has also been replaced by a more advanced one of Chinese origin that includes an advanced missile approach warning system (MAWS).

In terms of armament, the J-11B is compatible with a range of Chinese-designed weapons, including medium-range PL-12 air-to-air missiles (AAMs)

with active radar guidance and PL-8B infrared-guided AAMs.

Combat trainer version

While China never appears to have secured a licence to assemble or manufacture the two-seat Su-27UBK, it has developed its own combat trainer version of the J-11B, known as the J-11BS. This was likely achieved by reverse-engineering the Su-27UBK and updating it to J-11B standard. At the same time, the J-11BS introduced an all-new new digital fly-by-wire flight control system.

Other J-11B variants include the J-11BH, a land-based fighter for the People's Liberation Army Navy (PLAN). The J-11BSH, meanwhile, is the PLAN's land-based equivalent of the J-11B combat trainer.

Very few details are available about the number of J-11Bs that have been built. Most reliable sources suggest the total number of single-seat J-11Bs is around 150–160, together with around 100–120 of the two-seat J-11BS. Even before J-11B production ended, work seems to have begun on a mid-life update of the aircraft known as the J-11BG (or J-11BGH in naval service).

This was first reported in late 2019, and the first examples were characterized by their white (rather than black) radomes, suggesting that a new radar has been fitted, probably an advanced active electronically scanned array (AESA) type. The new short-range PL-10 AAM also appears to be included in the upgrade package.

FIGHTERS & INTERCEPTORS

THE MYSTERIOUS J-11D

Very little is known about the aircraft known as the J-11D, beyond the fact that it appears to be the final iteration of the prolific J-11 series. Some sources erroneously describe it as an electronic warfare variant (based on the J-11D nomenclature). In reality, however, it is a further upgrade of the J-11, but with significant structural changes, as well as uprated WS-10 engines, a digital fly-by-wire flight control system and new avionics, including an AESA radar.

Externally, the J-11D has a reshaped radome (see photograph), while other changes include an inflight refuelling probe installed on the port side of the nose and the IRST/laser rangefinder housing offset to starboard as found on the J-16. Once again, greater use is thought to be made of composite materials, further reducing airframe weight. The wings feature an additional pair of pylons for a maximum of 12 AAMs, including the latest medium-range PL-15s and short-range PL-10s.

Shenyang J-11B

This J-11B, coded 10320, is from the first production batch and retains the Lyulka A-31F engines. On its wing tip pylons it carries PL-8 infra-red homing missiles and, under its wings, PL-12 active radar guided air-to-air missiles. It is believed to have been assigned to the 1st Fighter Division, 1st Regiment, which became part of the Northern Theatre Command in 2011.

Shenyang J-11B

Weight (maximum take-off): 33,000kg (72,753lb)
Dimensions: Length: 21.9m (69ft 6in), Wingspan 14.7m (48ft 3in), Height 5.92m (19ft 5in)
Powerplant: Two Shenyang WS-10A 'Taihang' afterburning turbofans, 132kN (30,000lbf) thrust each (Block 02)
Maximum speed: Mach 2.35 (2500km/h, 1553mph)
Range: 3530km (2190 mi, 1,910 nmi)
Ceiling: 19,000m (62,000ft)
Crew: 1
Armament: One 30mm (1.18in) Gryazev-Shipunov GSh-30-1 cannon; 10 hardpoints: two under fuselage, two under air ducts, four under wings, four on wing-tips, with provisions for PL-12 and PL-15 missiles

FIGHTERS & INTERCEPTORS

Shenyang J-16

The J-16 seems to have originated in Chinese plans to develop an indigenous two-seat 'Strike Flanker' in preference to buying further batches of Su-30MKKs or Su-30MK2s from Russia.

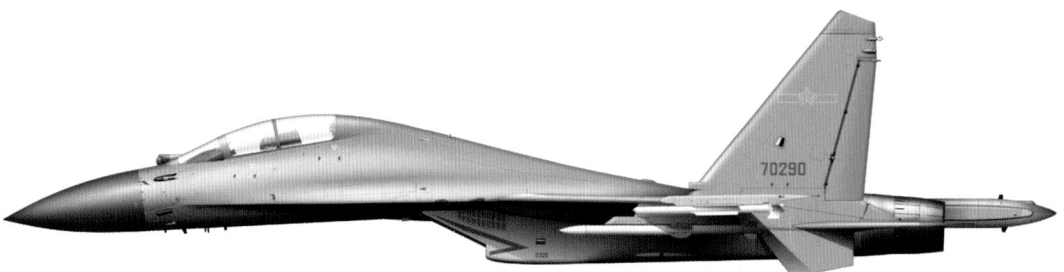

Shenyang J-16
This J-16 is from the Eastern Command's 98th Air Brigade based at Chongqing. She is coded 70290, making her "grey 20" and carrying the serial 0320 on her intakes. This multirole fighter is armed with a PL-10 imaging infra-red air-to-air missile on the wingtip and a PL-15 extended-range, active radar guided air-to-air missile beneath its wings.

Shenyang J-16
Weight (maximum take-off): 35,000kg (77,162lb)
Dimensions: Length: 21.9m (69ft 6in), Wingspan 14.7m (48ft 3in), Height 6.36m (20ft 9in)
Powerplant: Two Shenyang WS-10B afterburning turbofans, 135kN (30,000lbf) with afterburner
Maximum speed: Mach 2
Range: 3530km (2190 mi, 1,910 nmi)
Ceiling: 19,000m (62,000ft)
Crew: 2
Armament: One 30mm (1.18in) Gryazev-Shipunov GSh-30-1 cannon with 150 rounds; munitions on 12 external hardpoints

To achieve this goal, the J-16 ultimately emerged as a combination of the airframe of the two-seat J-11BS (itself a reverse-engineered Su-27UBK) and the domestically developed avionics and WS-10 series engines from the J-11B. Notably, the J-16 not only represents an apparent complete break from any previous 'Flanker' licence production agreements that may have existed with Russia but also fully embodies the advances and true multirole capability that China had long sought to incorporate into its J-11 fleet.

Prototype debut
The J-16 first appeared in July 2012, at that time still in prototype form. Very little is known about the test programme, but the aircraft is rumoured to have first flown on 17 October 2011. Thereafter, it seems likely that series production commenced by late 2013, although it was not until mid-2015 that the type was confirmed as being in PLAAF service. Outwardly, the J-16 may look similar to the Russian Su-30MKK, but it is understood to be very different under the skin, including a much greater use of modern composite materials in its construction. This is in addition to the more advanced avionics that are central to its overall efficiency as a weapon system but remain otherwise little-known.

Aesthetic traits
At a more superficial level, distinguishing features of the J-16 include an inflight refuelling probe installed on the port side of the nose and the infrared search and track (IRST)/laser rangefinder housing offset to starboard (as later adopted on the J-11D). The J-16 also has twin-wheel nose gear to cope with its increased weight, and taller vertical tail fins that likely contain additional fuel. The J-16

FIGHTERS & INTERCEPTORS

is powered by WS-10B turbofans as standard, reflecting the final maturity of the Chinese engine design.

At the heart of the J-16's revised avionics suite is a new active electronically scanned array (AESA) radar concealed below a new grey-painted radome without a pitot probe. Little is known about the radar and its capabilities, although it clearly provides for fully multirole capabilities. The radar is complemented by new electronic warfare self-protection systems, while the cockpit, although rarely seen, is similarly modernized. The J-16's crew are provided with panoramic touchscreen multifunction displays (MFDs) – apparently two for each pilot – and the cockpit is compatible with night-vision goggles as well as helmet-mounted displays. Other new avionics items include the indigenous BeiDou satellite navigation system, which features an antenna mounted on the spine.

Versatile carrier

Reflecting its multirole capabilities, the J-16 can carry a very wide range of Chinese-made precision-guided weapons. In the air-to-air domain, the aircraft can be armed with medium-range PL-15 and short-range PL-10 air-to-air missiles (AAMs), while a very

A Shenyang J-16 fighter at the 14th China International Aviation and Aerospace Exhibition, November 2022, in Zhuhai, Guangdong Province, China. This viewpoint offers a clear view of the engine air intakes.

FIGHTERS & INTERCEPTORS

large ultra-long-range AAM, apparently designated PL-17, has also been seen under test on the J-16. Targets on land and at sea can be engaged using the KD-88 air-to-surface missile, YJ-83K anti-ship missile and YJ-91 anti-radiation missile, to name just three of the most common weapons. The J-16 can also carry Chinese-made laser-guided bombs including from the LS-500 and JG-500 series.

These weapons are often carried in conjunction with electronic warfare and targeting pods. The typical electronic countermeasures store is the KG700 pod, while an advanced targeting pod – similar in appearance to the US-made Sniper pod – can be carried underneath one of the engine intakes.

In PLAAF service, the 'Strike Flanker' has emerged as the logical successor to the JH-7, as well as to earlier Su-27/J-11 versions. Since it was first noted as being in service in mid-2015, the J-16 has also undergone some improvements as production has continued. The second production batch, for example, was reportedly fitted with an improved type of AESA radar, and later series also began to receive low-visibility markings and insignia.

During production, additional offensive weapons were added to the J-16's armoury and improved engines were also installed. The latest powerplant comprises WS-10B Series

Shenyang J-16
This J-16, coded 61249, serves with the 3rd Brigade of the Northern Command, based at Qiqihar. It carries the serial number 0724 on its intakes, which feed its WS-10A engines. The aircraft has empty missile rails on its wingtips and a pair of rocket pods, carried side-by-side on a single pylon, under its wings. Each pod contains five 122mm (4.8in) folding fin unguided rockets.

03 turbofans, which feature longer exhaust nozzle 'feathers' of a slightly different design.

Drone controller
Although unconfirmed, it seems that the PLAAF is also experimenting with using the J-16 as a 'drone controller' aircraft. In this way, it's likely that the back-seater is able to use artificial intelligence to command unmanned aerial vehicles (UAVs) as part of collaborative missions.

The production numbers for the J-16 remain a matter of some debate. Authoritative sources suggest that, by the end of 2022, at least 220 examples were in PLAAF service. With production continuing, the J-16 is now the most numerous 'Flanker' variant in Chinese service and, with the exception of the stealthy J-20, the PLAAF's most capable tactical warplane.

FIGHTERS & INTERCEPTORS

J-16D FOR ELECTRONIC WARFARE

In something of a parallel to the US Navy's EA-18G Growler, which is based on the two-seat F/A-18F Super Hornet, China has developed a dedicated electronic warfare version of the J-16, known as the J-16D, albeit land-based rather than carrier-compatible. Like the EA-18G, the J-16D is equipped for suppression of enemy air defences (SEAD) missions and is thought to have made its first flight in prototype form in late 2015.

While retaining the basic airframe of the J-16, the J-16D features several notable modifications for its new mission. Most obvious are the very large wingtip pods, which likely contain electronic support measures (ESM) or electronic intelligence (ELINT) equipment. Around its airframe, the J-16D also features several additional electronic warfare antennas, aerials and dielectric panels. A reconfigured radome is thought to accommodate a different AESA radar optimized for electronic warfare. At the same time, the usual cannon and IRST/laser rangefinder housing have apparently been removed from the aircraft's nose.

As well as internal equipment, the J-16D can carry an array of specially developed electronic warfare pods below the wings and engine intakes. At least three of these pods have so far been identified, and they are likely mainly concerned with jamming across different portions of the radio-magnetic spectrum. For lethal SEAD, it's assumed that the J-16D can be armed with YJ-91 missiles and possibly also newly developed anti-radiation missiles.

The J-16D programme has been conducted with a greater degree of secrecy than most other Chinese 'Flanker' variants, but by early 2019, it was apparent that the aircraft was ready to enter PLAAF service. An official public debut for the J-16D was followed by an appearance in the static display at the Zhuhai Airshow in September 2021.

Shenyang J-16D
Weight (maximum take-off): 35,000kg (77,162lb)
Dimensions: Length: 21.9m (69ft 6in), Wingspan 14.7m (48ft 3in), Height 6.36m (20ft 9in)
Powerplant: Two Shenyang WS-10B afterburning turbofans, 135kN (30,000lbf) with afterburner
Maximum speed: Mach 2
Range: 3530km (2190 mi, 1,910 nmi)
Ceiling: 19,000m (62,000ft)
Crew: 2
Armament: Equipped with wingtip EW pods; munitions on 12 external hardpoints, with provisions for YJ-91 anti-shipping missiles

Shenyang J-16D
This J-16D was displayed at the Zhuhai International Airshow in September 2021. She is uncoded but carries the serial 0109 on the intakes. The wingtips carry the diagnostic ICM pods of the type and, on pylons beneath the wings and intake cheeks, are various jamming pods from the RKZ930 family. A pair of missiles, reported to be PL-15s, are carried in tandem on the belly centreline.

Chengdu J-20

Apparently assigned the Western reporting name 'Firefang', the Chengdu J-20, known in China as 'Mighty Dragon', is the third stealth fighter to have entered service anywhere in the world, a major accomplishment for China's aerospace industry and a key part of the ongoing modernization of the PLAAF.

The early years of the J-20 programme are shrouded in mystery, but work seems to have been started by the mid-1990s, with an official announcement of the existence of the so-called Project 718 coming from US intelligence in 1997. At this stage, the programme aimed to provide the PLAAF with a new-generation twin-engine heavy fighter, and both Chengdu and Shenyang were involved, offering competing designs. As far as is known, the Shenyang proposal was more conservative, with the company's No. 601 Institute coming up with a 'tri-plane' concept that included canard foreplanes, widely canted tailfins and horizontal tailplanes.

Radical design

Ultimately, Beijing opted for a more radical design from Chengdu's No. 611 Institute. This is based on a delta planform with canard foreplanes and widely canted, all-moving tailfins. While there are no horizontal tailplanes, there are twin ventral stabilizing fins mounted on the tail booms. The engine intakes are also of a notably advanced design, with diverterless supersonic inlets (DSI), which help contribute to the aircraft's overall very low-observable (VLO) or stealth characteristics.

The appearance of the first J-20 prototype in late 2010 came as a surprise to most observers. It was followed by a maiden flight on 11 January 2011. The second prototype took to the air in 2012. However, the third prototype that emerged in late 2013 featured various modifications including several refinements that would be incorporated in the production aircraft.

First deliveries

Several more prototypes followed, and the first of the production J-20s were handed over to the PLAAF in December 2016. The initial deliveries were made to the PLAAF's flight test and training unit at the airbases of Dingxin and Cangzhou. Overall, it seems that the aircraft at Dingxin

---

Chengdu J-20A
Weight (maximum take-off): 37,013kg (81,600lb)
Dimensions: Length 20.4m (66ft 10in), Wingspan 13.5m (44ft 4in), Height 4.45m (14ft 7in)
Powerplant: Two Saturn AL-31FN turbofans each rated at 145kN (33,000lb) thrust with afterburning
Maximum speed: Mach 2.0+
Range: 3400km (2113 miles)
Ceiling: 20,000m (65,617ft)
Crew: 1
Armament: Disposable ordnance carried in one large weapon bay in the lower fuselage, typically comprising up to four PL-15 AAMs, plus two PL-10 AAMs carried in lateral weapon bays behind the intakes; optional additional ordnance on four underwing pylons

---

Chengdu J-20A
This J-20A serves with the PLAAF's 172nd Air Brigade, part of the Flight Test and Training Base, which operates from Cangzhou. This is one of two test and training units operating the J-20.

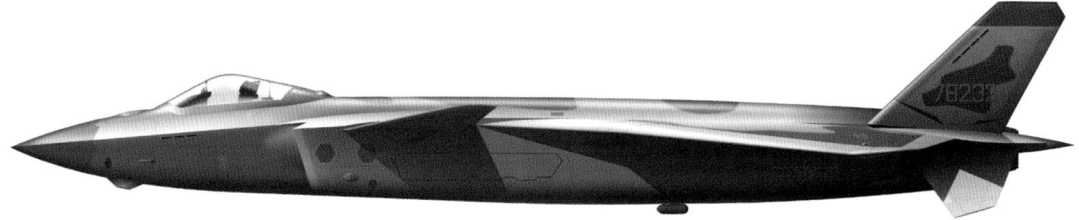

A Chengdu J-20 stealth fighter can climb at a rate of 304 metres (998ft) per second.

were tasked with developing and testing operational tactics for the J-20, while the Cangzhou unit was tasked with advanced training for pilots of the new aircraft.

In February 2018, the J-20 was officially declared 'combat ready', although it was January 2019 before the first operational frontline unit – the 9th Air Brigade at Wuhu under the Eastern Theatre Command – began to operate the aircraft.

Components and features

In common with other stealth fighters, the J-20's design is – to a significant degree – based around the internal carriage of its weapons. Altogether, the J-20 has three internal weapons bays: a large central weapons bay below the fuselage, which typically carries up to four active radar-guided PL-15 medium-range air-to-air missiles (AAMs) and two smaller lateral bays behind the intakes, each of which accommodates one infrared-guided PL-10 short-range AAM.

The J-20 incorporates an advanced avionics suite with an active electronically scanned array (AESA) Type 1475 radar at its core. The mission avionics also include an apparent distributed situational awareness system similar to the EODAS found on the US-made F-35 and an infrared search and track (IRST) system. The cockpit features a wide-angle holographic head-up display (HUD) and a touchscreen panoramic display.

The development of the J-20 has been greatly influenced by China's travails in developing reliable modern turbofan engines for its combat aircraft. From the start, it was likely planned to incorporate an indigenous powerplant in the form of the WS-15, although development of this engine was slow. This meant that the first J-20 prototypes and test aircraft were fitted with Russian-supplied AL-31FN engines.

As an interim solution, pending the availability of the definitive WS-15, the J-20 was then fitted with another Chinese engine, the WS-10, already proven in the J-11B and J-16. The first J-20 powered by the WS-10 was noted in September 2017, the engines now featuring characteristic serrated nozzle 'feathers'. Production of the WS-10-powered version of the aircraft, known as the J-20A, appears to have commenced by early 2019.

Meanwhile, there have been reports that the J-20 might receive engines with thrust-vectoring controls

FIGHTERS & INTERCEPTORS

for enhanced manoeuvrability, and perhaps in relation to this, a J-10B testbed fitted with a thrust-vectoring WS-10 began to be tested around 2018. There are rumours, too, that at least one of these thrust-vectoring engines has been tested on a J-20, but this cannot be confirmed.

More importantly, in July 2023, photos appeared suggesting that a J-20 was now being tested with two of the new WS-15 engines installed. Reliable accounts suggest that a production version of the aircraft fitted with these engines could be ready for service in 2025 or 2026. The new powerplant is expected to confer super-cruise performance and an enhanced level of manoeuvrability.

Refinements

In the meantime, production of the J-20A continues, with refinements also being added to the aircraft. In late 2022, for example, a modified version of the J-20A was noted under test at Chengdu. This variant features a slightly raised cockpit and a deeper spine, which likely contains additional avionics and perhaps also more fuel. At the same time, the nose of the aircraft has been slightly reprofiled, probably to reduce drag. Other changes have been made to the engine intakes, likely in order to accommodate the WS-15s. By late 2022, it was also assessed that total J-20 production had reached around 150 examples.

J-20S

Alongside further development of the single-seat aircraft, Chengdu has also tested a tandem two-seat version known as the J-20S, which first took to the air in November 2021 powered by WS-10 engines. At least two J-20S prototypes were under test by mid-2022, although the exact role envisaged for this version remains unclear. The two-seater appears to retain full combat capabilities, so is likely intended for operational use rather than just as a trainer. There has been speculation that it might eventually serve in a strike role with electronic warfare as a command-and-control node or perhaps even as a drone controller for a new generation of 'loyal wingman'-type unmanned combat aircraft.

It is expected that the J-20 will eventually begin to incorporate new weapons, likely including a new long-range AAM. This missile will almost

Chengdu J-20A

Weight (maximum take-off): 37,013kg (81,600lb)
Dimensions: Length 20.4m (66ft 10in), Wingspan 13.5m (44ft 4in), Height 4.45m (14ft 7in)
Powerplant: Two Saturn AL-31FN turbofans each rated at 145kN (33,000lb) thrust with afterburning
Maximum speed: Mach 2.0+
Range: 3400km (2113 miles)
Ceiling: 20,000m (65,617ft)
Crew: 1
Armament: Disposable ordnance carried in one large weapon bay in the lower fuselage, typically comprising up to four PL-15 AAMs, plus two PL-10 AAMs carried in lateral weapon bays behind the intakes; optional additional ordnance on four underwing pylons

Chengdu J-20A
J-20A serial number 78272 is among the aircraft assigned to the 176th Air Brigade at Dingxin, which also falls under the administrative control of the Flight Test and Training Base.

A Chengdu J-20 takes part in a fly past during the opening of Airshow China in Zhuhai, 2016.

certainly be designed specifically for internal carriage, allowing the aircraft to be armed with six medium-range missiles in its main weapons bay, as opposed to the current four. A Chinese equivalent to the US-made Small Diameter Bomb has also been suggested, allowing the J-20 to also undertake strike roles. Other offensive weapons for internal carriage are likely, perhaps including new air-to-ground missiles and anti-radiation missiles.

FIGHTERS & INTERCEPTORS

Sukhoi Su-27

The story of the 'Flanker' series of fighters in China starts with the original Su-27 'Flanker-B' or rather its Su-27SK export derivative, which Beijing acquired from the then Soviet Union together with the two-seat Su-27UBK, an export version of the Su-27UB 'Flanker-C' combat trainer.

Sukhoi Su-27SK 'Flanker B'
This Su-27SK is from the very first contract of 24, delivered to the PLAAF in 1991–92, based at Wuhu Wanli air base. On the wingtips are a pair of L005 Sorbtsiya Electronic Warfare pods. The serial number 13241 is made up of '13-4' to signify the unit/base, combined with the split '21', showing it to be the 21st airframe delivered. Blue bort numbers were standard at the time and it carries the original pale two-tone grey scheme.

The Soviet history of the Su-27 stretches all the way back to 1969 when the Perspektivnyi Frontovoi Istrebitel (Future Tactical Fighter) programme was launched to counter the F-15 Eagle. Sukhoi's T-10 design was chosen in 1971 and the prototype T-10-1 first flew on 20 May 1977. The original T-10 configuration proved disappointing, and after seven test aircraft, it was totally redesigned as the T-10S, which was first flown in April 1981. The T-10S was a great improvement and entered production as the Su-27, the first example of which took to the air in June 1982. A two-seat combat trainer variant known as the Su-27UB subsequently entered quantity production in 1986.

The Su-27 became one of the pre-eminent Soviet fighters of its generation, with official figures from Sukhoi claiming a total production run of 645 single-seat Su-27s between 1982 and 1999, after which production was rapidly drawn down. As a result, it is estimated that around 660 single-seaters were built along with 190 Su-27UB/UBK two-seaters.

China became the first export customer for the Su-27 and the only foreign nation to place an order for the type before the demise of the Soviet Union. As well as buying aircraft from the Soviet (later Russian) production lines, Beijing also secured a license production agreement to build single-seat Su-27s under the J-11 designation. With the Su-27, China finally secured a modern fourth-generation fighter and a substitute for the advanced version of the J-8, with Western avionics, after that programme was cancelled as a result of political tensions in 1989.

By late 1989, the Soviet Union was actively courting China as a potential customer for its high-end defence products, including fighters. In May 1990, a Chinese delegation arrived in Moscow to discuss a purchase of fighters. At this stage, both the Su-27 and the smaller and less complex Mikoyan MiG-29 were in the running.

Arms delivery agreement
In June 1990, China and the Soviet Union signed an agreement covering 'mutual arms deliveries', although it wasn't until several weeks or even months later that the Su-27 was formalized as part of the deal. The political and geo-strategic turmoil of this time also had an effect on the Su-27 deal. In Russia, the failed coup attempt in 1990 led to delays in the programme. Soon after, the 1991 Gulf War demonstrated to China the importance of securing an advanced new type of fighter like the Su-27.

Ultimately, China acquired Su-27s under three separate contracts. The first of these, dated March 1991, was reportedly valued at more than US$1 billion and covered 24 aircraft, as well as related armament, logistics and pilot training. The contract itself was signed in November 1991, by which time the first group of PLAAF fighter pilots began training on the type in Russia. Deliveries of the first batch of aircraft

FIGHTERS & INTERCEPTORS

Sukhoi Su-27SK
Weight (maximum take-off): 28,300kg (62,391lb)
Dimensions: Length 21.94m (72ft) without probe, Wingspan 14.7m (48ft 3in), Height 5.93m (19ft 6in)
Powerplant: Two Saturn AL-31F turbofans each rated at 122.58kN (27,558lb) thrust with afterburning
Maximum speed: Mach 2.35
Range: 3720km (2312 miles)
Ceiling: 18,500m (60,700ft)
Crew: 1
Armament: One GSh-301 30mm (1.1in) cannon, plus up to 4430kg (9766lb) of external stores on 10 weapons pylons

Chinese Air Force Colonel Wang Wei and the Chairman of the Joint Chiefs of Staff, US Marine Corps General Peter Pace, talk "air power" while examining the cockpit of a PLAAF Su-27 'Flanker' at Anshan Airfield, China, 2007.

FIGHTERS & INTERCEPTORS

Sukhoi Su-27SK 'Flanker B'
This Su-27SK is in the later, darker, grey scheme and belongs to the 6th Regiment of the 2nd Division, whose badge appears on the fin, based at Suixi air base around 2005. Coded 16039, 'Blue 609', is another of the imported Su-27s and carries R-27 medium-range air-to-air missiles (AA-10 Alamo B) on the intake pylons and short range R-73 missiles (AA-11 Archer) missiles on the outer wing pylons.

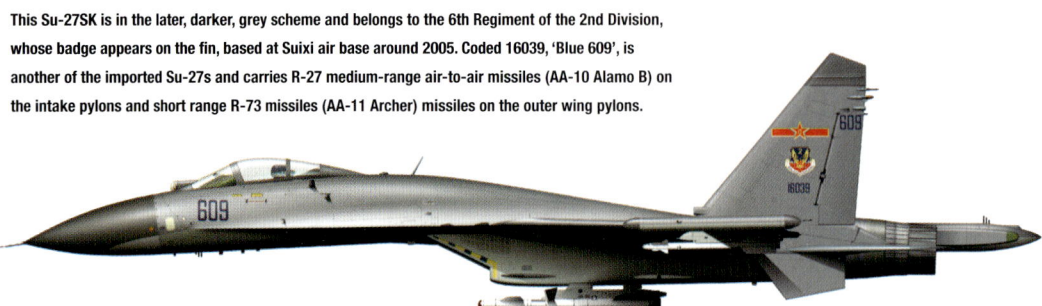

began in June 1992, when eight Su-27SKs and four Su-27UBKs arrived at Wuhu air base, in Anhui Province. The remaining 12 Su-27SKs were delivered the same year.

Second and third orders
Another batch of 24 Su-27s was covered by a second contract, signed in May 1995. This time, it comprised 16 single-seat Su-27SK and eight two-seat Su-27UBK aircraft. Deliveries began in April 1996. The third and final contract for Su-27s was signed in December 1999 after the contract for licence manufacturing of the J-11 had been agreed. Since the local assembly and manufacture would (according to the contract) be limited to single-seaters, the third batch of aircraft from Russian production were all two-seat Su-27UBK aircraft. Reportedly, deliveries also began in December 1999. There has been much speculation about the exact configuration of the Su-27s bought by China, although they look outwardly similar. Reports suggest that changes to the Chinese aircraft include an increased maximum take-off weight and strengthened undercarriage, allowing an expanded weapons load.

There are suggestions, too, that the final batch of Su-27UBKs acquired in 1999 were completed to a more advanced standard, with an improved radar allowing the use of the R-77 (AA-12 'Adder') active-radar air-to-air missile (AAM).

Otherwise, multiple claims suggest the Su-27SK's radar and electro-optical sighting system are 'downgraded export variants', although it seems aircraft in later delivery batches also had R-77 missile capability.

Currently, the first-generation Su-27 is a dwindling power within the PLAAF, superseded by locally produced J-11s and more advanced 'Flanker' versions. Almost certainly, some of the earlier Su-27SK aircraft have already been withdrawn from service, although there are also Western accounts that suggest that Su-27SKs now fly within mixed units alongside J-11As.

Sukhoi Su-27UBK 'Flanker C'
Weight (maximum take-off): 30,500kg (67241lb)
Dimensions: Length 21.94m (72ft) without probe, Wingspan 14.7m (48ft 3in), Height 5.93m (19ft 6in)
Powerplant: Two Saturn AL-31F turbofans, each rated at 122.58kN (27,558lb) thrust with afterburning
Maximum speed: Mach 2
Range: 3000km (1864 miles)
Ceiling: 17,500m (57,415ft)
Crew: 2
Armament: One GSh-301 30mm (1.2in) cannon, plus up to 4430kg (9766lb) of external stores on 10 weapons pylons

Sukhoi Su-27UBK 'Flanker C'
Sukhoi Su-27UBK, bort no Blue 28, serial number 16238, identifies this aircraft as belonging to the 6th Regiment of the 2nd Division, based at Suixi in the late 1990s. This trainer is unarmed, aside from the wingtip EW pod, and wears the early light blue grey scheme.

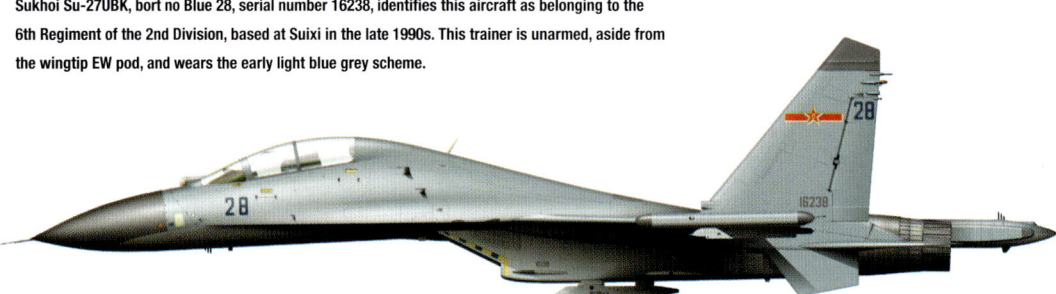

Sukhoi Su-30

Collectively known in the West as the 'Flanker-G', the Su-30MKK and Su-30MK2, acquired by China, are two-seat multirole versions of the original Su-27 optimized for long-range strike missions.

While only the Su-30MKK is currently flown by the PLAAF, both the Su-30MKK and the Su-30MK2 have their roots in a Soviet-era initiative to develop a long-range interceptor based on the airframe of the two-seat Su-27UB 'Flanker-C' combat trainer.

Origins

Optimized for use by the Soviet Air Defence Forces, development of what was initially known as the Su-27PU began in 1986 – the designation was later changed to Su-30. Major changes compared with the Su-27UB included a full fire-control system, a large tactical situation display in the rear cockpit and an inflight refuelling probe. The first Su-30 prototype took to the air on 30 December 1989, but only a handful of production aircraft were ever completed for Russia.

Thereafter, development of the Su-30 family was continued primarily for export, and this work followed two distinct lines. At the Irkutsk factory, the Su-30MK series included canard foreplanes, a digital fly-by-wire system, thrust-vectoring engines and an open-architecture fire-control system based around the Bars electronically scanned radar.

Less advanced version

Meanwhile, in Komsomolsk-on-Amur in the Russian Far East, the Komsomolsk-on-Amur Aircraft Production Association (KnAAPO) worked on its own Su-30. This was somewhat less advanced than the Irkutsk version, lacking the canard foreplanes and open-architecture fire-control system and having less sophisticated radar options.

China became the first export customer for the KnAAPO Su-30 when it ordered the Su-30MKK. Here, the designation signifies *Modernizirovannyi Kommercheskiy Kitayski*, or 'modernized commercial for China'.

In Russia, the development of the multirole Su-30MK series coincided with renewed PLAAF interest in a

---

Sukhoi Su-30MKK

Weight (maximum take-off): 24,500kg (54,013lb)
Dimensions: Length 21.2m (69ft 6in) without probe, Wingspan 14.7m (48ft 3in), Height 5.72m (18ft 9in)
Powerplant: Two modified AL-31F series 3 turbofans, each rated at 122.5kN (27,558lb) with afterburning
Maximum speed: Mach 2.17
Range: 3000km (1864 miles)
Ceiling: 17,000m (55,775ft)
Crew: 2
Armament: One GSh-301 30mm (1.2in) cannon, plus up to 6500kg (14,330lb) of stores carried on 12 hardpoints

---

Sukhoi Su-30MKK
This Su-30MKK belongs to the 54th Regiment of the 18th Division based at Changsha, serial number 20694, becoming "Yellow 64". It is one of several aircraft to receive an 'aggressor' scheme for disimilar air combat training in 2012.

FIGHTERS & INTERCEPTORS

Two Su-30 fighters take off from Guangzhou, China, August 2016. PLAAF aircraft, including H-6K bombers and Su-30 fighters, completed a patrol of airspace above the Nansha and Huangyan islands in the South China Sea, as part of actual combat training to improve the PLAAF's response to security threats.

Sukhoi Su-30MKK
This Sukhoi Su-30MKK, coded 66155, 'Yellow 15', belongs to the 54th Brigade, based out of Changsha Air Base in September 2020. It is armed with Vympel R-73 (AA-11 Archer) air-to-ship and R-27 (AA-10 Alamo-A) air-to-air underwing missiles and EW pods on its wing tips. It is in the current gunship grey scheme, with the unit's eagle motif beneath the cockpit.

FIGHTERS & INTERCEPTORS

more capable fourth-generation fighter that would be optimized for longer-range offensive missions, using precision-guided munitions of the kinds that were still available to China only in very modest numbers. Adding to the urgency was the general disappointment with the indigenous JH-7 strike aircraft and the limited capacity to adapt the locally built J-11 as a multirole platform.

Russia–China deal

Beijing and Moscow began talks about the sale of a Su-30MK derivative in 1996. At the end of that year, a purchase agreement valued at $1.85 billion was signed covering 38 aircraft. At this stage, it was not yet clear where the aircraft would be built, but in December 1997, Sukhoi selected the KnAAPO plant, apparently because Irkutsk was already busy building the Su-30MKI for India.

Designed by Sukhoi and built by KnAAPO, the Su-30MKK utilized components from various members of the 'Flanker' family, including the two-seat forward fuselage of the Su-30, while other parts of the fuselage and tail came from the single-seat Su-27M. Yet more parts came from the original single-seat Su-27, while the strengthened undercarriage came from the Su-30MKI.

Improved specs

The beefed-up landing gear (including twin-wheel nose gear) is required to cope with an increased maximum take-off weight. This means the aircraft can carry a full internal fuel load as well as the maximum 8000kg (17,637lb) external stores payload on 12 hardpoints. To reduce airframe weight, a greater proportion of composite materials is incorporated. The Su-30MKK also uses a modern fly-by-wire control system with quadruple redundancy.

In terms of avionics, the Su-30MKK is fitted with an N001VE radar, which has improved air-to-air capabilities and enhanced air-to-ground resolution. The radar can track 10 aerial targets, and engage two of them, simultaneously. It is allied with a new OLS-30 infrared search and track (IRST) system and a

---

Sukhoi Su-30MKK

Weight (maximum take-off): 24,500kg (54,013lb)
Dimensions: Length 21.2m (69ft 6in) without probe, Wingspan 14.7m (48ft 3in), Height 5.72m (18ft 9in)
Powerplant: Two modified AL-31F series 3 turbofans, each rated at 122.5kN (27,558lb) with afterburning
Maximum speed: Mach 2.17
Range: 3000km (1864 miles)
Ceiling: 17,000m (55,775ft)
Crew: 2
Armament: One GSh-301 30mm (1.2in) cannon, plus up to 6500kg (14,330lb) of stores carried on 12 hardpoints

helmet-mounted sight. The two-person crew is provided with an all-digital cockpit, with a pair of large colour LCD screens for each.

The new aircraft is able to carry a much wider range of weapons, including the active radar-homing R-77 (AA-12 'Adder') air-to-air missile (AAM) as well as air-to-surface stores, such as the Kh-29 (AS-14 'Kedge') series of air-to-ground missiles, the Kh-31P (AS-17 'Krypton') anti-radiation missile and the Kh-59ME (AS-18 'Kazoo') air-to-ground missile with standoff capability. The aircraft can also be armed with TV-guided bombs including the 500kg (1102lb) KAB-500Kr and the 1500kg (3307lb) KAB-1500Kr. After two experimental airframes had been completed to test certain subsystems, the first true Su-30MKK prototype took to the air on 20 May 1999.

According to an agreement signed between China and Russia in 1999, all 38 aircraft were to be delivered between 2000 and 2001. In December 2000, the first batch of 10 Su-30MKKs was officially handed over to the PLAAF in Russia and then delivered to China. All 38 had been delivered by the end of 2001, and the first unit to receive the aircraft was the 9th Air Regiment at Wuhu, part of the 3rd Air Division.

Second batch for China
Apparently satisfied with the Su-30MKK, China signed a contract in July 2001 to order a second batch of 38. Deliveries of these aircraft began between August and December 2002, and the last examples arrived in China in October 2003. While the first 76 Su-30MKKs were delivered to the PLAAF,

the third contract, signed in January 2003, covered 24 examples of a specific naval strike variant – known as the Su-30MK2 – for the People's Liberation Army Navy. Key to this version is its ability to employ anti-ship missiles and its more advanced radar.

As such, the Su-30MK2 is equipped with an upgraded N001VEP radar compatible with the Kh-31A anti-shipping version of the AS-17 'Krypton' and can attack two targets simultaneously. Other anti-ship missile options include the Kh-59MK. Deliveries of the Su-30MK2 to the PLAN's 4th Division, 10th Air Regiment had been completed by the end of August 2004.

This PLAAF Sukhoi Su-30MKK, serial number 78033, is shown at Lipetsk Air Base in Russia, during joint exercises.

FIGHTERS & INTERCEPTORS

SU-30 UPGRADE

Since their service entry, some efforts have been made to improve the capabilities of the Su-30MKK and Su-30MK2, including adding GPS/BeiDou navigation equipment, the indigenous KG600/KL700 electronic countermeasures pod and the PL-12 AAM, although the latter missile is likely only available to the naval 'Flanker-G'.

The Su-30MKK remains one of the most important assets for the PLAAF, chiefly due to its ability to fly long distances and penetrate contested airspace before delivering powerful munitions against air and ground targets. Making use of its aerial refuelling capability, the Su-30MKK can undertake missions far out into the South China Sea or East China Sea, for example, and can provide long-range escort for H-6 bombers.

Long-term, however, it seems the status of the Su-30MKK with the PLAAF may not be so secure, especially since the J-16 is now available in larger numbers and has, from the start, fully Chinese avionics and weapons options.

Sukhoi Su-35

The Su-35, known by the Western reporting name 'Flanker-E', is the latest and most advanced version of the 'Flanker' family to enter Russian service, and this multirole fighter has also been offered for export.

Considering Shenyang's own developments of the basic aircraft, including the multirole J-16, it was a notable surprise when Beijing also decided to buy a batch of Su-35s from Russia.

Today's Su-35 traces its lineage back to Soviet-era plans to develop a much-improved version of the single-seat Su-27 'Flanker-B' then poised to enter service. These plans began around 1982. Then, in late 1993, Moscow directed Sukhoi to begin development of the aircraft, then known as the Su-27M (or, within Sukhoi, as the T-10M).

Sukhoi Su-35
This Su-35, serial number 61271, 'Yellow 21', is shown as seen at Novosibirsk Tolmachevo Airport in Siberia in May 2018, reportedly as a stopover before flying onto Zhukovsky, either for an upgrade or for pilot training.

Specs and materials

Key features of the advanced 'Flanker' would include a new multifunction phased-array radar that would offer multirole capabilities, while aerodynamic changes included canard foreplanes for improved manoeuvrability. The aircraft also featured a strengthened undercarriage

Sukhoi Su-35
Weight (maximum take-off): 34,500kg (76,059lb)
Dimensions: Length 21.9m (71ft 10in), Wingspan 14.7m (48ft 2in), Height 5.9m (19ft 4in)
Powerplant: Two Saturn AL-41F-1S thrust-vectoring turbofans each rated at 137.3kN (30,865lb) thrust with afterburning
Maximum speed: Mach 2.25
Range: 3000km (1864 miles)
Ceiling: 18,000m (59,055ft)
Crew: 1
Armament: One GSh-301 30mm (1.2in) cannon, plus up to 8000kg (17,637lb) of stores carried on 12 hardpoints

FIGHTERS & INTERCEPTORS

(with twin-wheel nose gear), taller vertical tail fins and an inflight refuelling probe. Construction would make greater use of composite materials to reduce overall airframe weight and bulk.

The Su-27M first took to the air on 28 June 1988. After 12 aircraft were completed for test work, the first production examples were completed in 1995 (now with the designation Su-35). Only a handful of these aircraft were ever procured for Russian service, and with no meaningful interest from the Russian Ministry of Defence for the time being, the focus turned to possible exports.

Sukhoi relaunch

However, the original Su-35 also failed to receive any foreign orders. For a while, the project appeared to be dead. However, in the early 2000s, Sukhoi relaunched the programme, now offering what was known as the Su-35BM (Bolshaya Modernisatsiya, meaning 'big modernization'). With delays to the new-generation Su-57 fighter, Russia placed an order for a version of the Su-35 (the BM suffix by now having been dropped). The production version for the Russian Aerospace Forces is known as the Su-35S and was first ordered in 2009.

While the exact reasons behind China's acquisition of the Su-35 remain unclear, Beijing reportedly began to show interest in the aircraft in the mid-2000s. After protracted negotiations, China and Russia agreed a deal for the sale of 24 of the aircraft in November 2015. The deal was reportedly valued at around $2 billion, with production to be handled by the Komsomolsk-on-Amur Aircraft Production Association (KnAAPO).

Features of the Su-35

While China was already engaged in its own advanced 'Flanker' programme with the two-seat multirole J-16, the Su-35 nevertheless offered several features that were likely of particular interest to the PLAAF. In particular, the Su-35 is equipped with AL-41F-1S (117S) turbofan engines incorporating thrust-vectoring nozzles used in conjunction with a quadruplex digital fly-by-wire flight control system for a very high level of manoeuvrability. In terms of avionics, the N135 Irbis-E passive electronically scanned array (PESA) radar was likely also especially interesting to the PLAAF.

Sukhoi Su-35
Weight (maximum take-off): 34,500kg (76,059lb)
Dimensions: Length 21.9m (71ft 10in), Wingspan 14.7m (48ft 2in), Height 5.9m (19ft 4in)
Powerplant: Two Saturn AL-41F-1S thrust-vectoring turbofans each rated at 137.3kN (30,865lb) thrust with afterburning
Maximum speed: Mach 2.25
Range: 3000km (1864 miles)
Ceiling: 18,000m (59,055ft)
Crew: 1
Armament: One GSh-301 30mm (1.2in) cannon, plus up to 8000kg (17,637lb) of stores carried on 12 hardpoints

---

Sukhoi Su-35
Serial number 61272, 'Yellow 22', is armed with Vympel R-73 (AA-11 Archer) air-to-ship and R-27 (AA-10 Alamo-A) air-to-air underwing missiles and carries wing tip EW pods. It was photographed while escorting a Xian H-6K bomber over the Bashi Channel, Philippines, in May 2018.

A PLAAF Sukhoi Su-35 jet fighter lands at Zhukovsky airport, Moscow region, Russia, May 2018.

The Irbis-E radar has a track-while-scan capability of up to 30 air targets. Eight of these targets can be engaged simultaneously using medium-range active-radar air-to-air missiles (AAMs). As well as air-to-air engagements, the radar has an air-to-ground mode in which it can simultaneously engage four surface targets. Maximum radar detection range against aerial targets is reportedly in the region of 400km (249 miles).

The Irbis-E is used as part of a new fire control system complex, which also integrates the OLS-35 infrared search and track (IRST) system with thermal imaging and TV cameras plus a laser rangefinder and target designator. Using the OLS-35, the pilot can track four aerial targets simultaneously. The Su-35 also features a notably advanced self-protection suite, including the Pastel radar warning receiver (RWR) that can be used to cue targets for anti-radiation missiles.

Self-protection is also entrusted to an electro-optical missile-approach warning suite, with six ultraviolet sensors located around the airframe, laser warning sensors and Khibiny-M electronic countermeasures (ECM) pods carried on the wingtips.

Usage by China

The first four Su-35s were delivered to China in December 2016, followed by two further batches of 10 in 2017 and 2019. On arrival, the PLAAF's new Su-35s touched down at Cangzhou/Cangxian, but they were ultimately deployed to Suixi, within the Southern Theatre Command, where they are operated by the 2nd Fighter Division, 6th Air Regiment, a unit that was later redesignated as the 6th Air Brigade. From here, the aircraft regularly operate as long-range fighter escorts for H-6K bombers, including missions close to Taiwan and over the South China Sea.

Operational Chinese Su-35s have only even been noted as carrying Russian-supplied weapons and stores, primarily the R-77-1 (AA-12 'Adder') and R-73/74 (AA-11 'Archer') AAMs, as well as Khibiny-M ECM pods.

BOMBERS & ATTACK AIRCRAFT

BOMBERS & ATTACK AIRCRAFT

As of the mid-2020s, aerospace and military observers are looking forward to the long-awaited appearance of China's new strategic bomber, likely designated H-20, and very probably a stealthy flying-wing design comparable to the US Air Force's B-21 Raider. In the meantime, the more capable versions of the H-6 continue to provide the backbone of the PLAAF strategic bomber fleet, mainly carrying stand-off cruise missiles and supported at a tactical level by the JH-7 strike aircraft, which is also optimized for maritime operations.

- Xi'an H-6
- Xi'an JH-7

A Xi'an H-6K strategic bomber, serial number 20119, seen at Dyagilevo air base during the Aviadarts 2018 competition, Russia.

BOMBERS & ATTACK AIRCRAFT

Xi'an H-6

Today, the Xi'an H-6, known by the Western reporting name 'Badger', is the only 'heavy' bomber in Chinese service. Remarkably, considering that it is based on a design that dates from the late 1940s, the H-6 remains in limited production to this day.

The story of the H-6 can be traced back to the period of close relations between China and the Soviet Union in the 1950s. With the PLAAF seeking to establish a more capable bomber fleet, in September 1957, Moscow approved the establishment of a production line for a licenced version of its Tupolev Tu-16 in China.

To help facilitate this, Tupolev provided China with two Tu-16 pattern aircraft in early 1959, after which further aircraft were supplied in kit form for assembly in Harbin. As early as September 1959, the first Chinese-assembled aircraft, known locally as the H-6, made its maiden flight.

Nuclear test

From a very early stage, China wanted the H-6 to form part of the country's strategic nuclear forces, and one aircraft was modified for the carriage of a Chinese-made freefall nuclear bomb, which was subsequently dropped at the Lop Nor test site in May 1965. In the meantime, however, relations with Moscow had soured, and the decision to relocate the production effort to Xi'an, allowing Harbin to focus its efforts on the H-5 light jet bomber, caused further upheavals for the programme. Ultimately, the effort required to move production meant the H-6 programme had to be effectively started again from scratch, and the first example built at Xi'an only took to the air in December 1968.

H-6As

The first Xi'an-built aircraft were known as H-6As, and these formed the basis of a range of specialist versions, including drone carriers, reconnaissance aircraft and electronic intelligence platforms. Most important were the nuclear-capable H-6E and the conventional H-6F bomber derivatives. H-6As remained in service into the mid-2010s thanks to various efforts to upgrade them with new navigation systems, electronic countermeasures (ECM) and electronic support measures (ESM) equipment.

H-6D/H

During the 1970s, further development of the aircraft began to focus on missile carriers, primarily for anti-

---

Xi'an H-6K

Weight (maximum take-off): 95,000kg (209,439lb)
Dimensions: Length 34.8m (114ft 2in), Wingspan 33m (108ft 3in), Height 10.36m (34ft)
Powerplant: Two Soloviev D-30KP-2 turbofan engines each rated at 118kN (27,000lb) thrust
Maximum speed: 1050km/h (650mph)
Range: 3500km (2200 miles)
Ceiling: 12,800m (42,000ft)
Crew: 4
Armament: Six underwing pylons for air-launched KD-20 or KD-63 land-attack cruise missiles

---

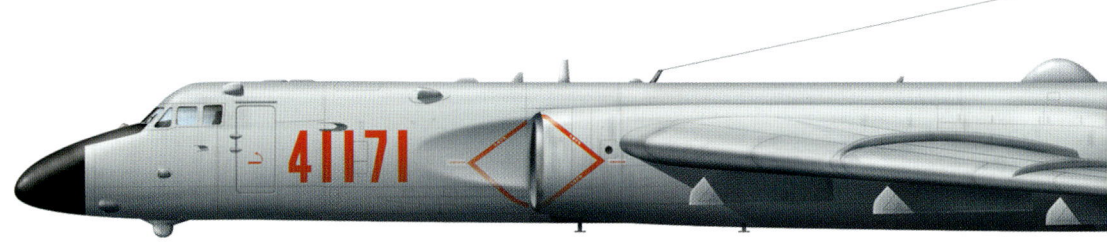

BOMBERS & ATTACK AIRCRAFT

shipping strikes. The H-6D was therefore intended for the People's Liberation Army Navy – Naval Aviation. This version featured two new hardpoints under the wings for YJ-6 missiles as well as a large navigation/attack radar. These aircraft saw extensive service, with survivors being converted to become H-6DU tankers (see box on page 48).

The H-6D served as the basis for successive missile carrier versions, including the PLAAF's H-6H, which operates in the land-attack role armed with a pair of TV-guided KD-63 cruise missiles. Defensive armament is deleted, and a new radome is fitted aft of the bomb bay.

The first prototype H-6H took to the air in late 1998 and it appears to have entered service around 2002. The PLAAF has since upgraded its H-6Hs, adding countermeasures launchers and radar warning receivers (RWR) as well as the KD-63H missile with infrared guidance.

H-6G

Meanwhile, the H-6G for the PLAN entered service around 2005. This is armed with four YJ-83K anti-ship missiles on underwing pylons and has a large navigation/attack radar below the nose. It also features a more capable self-defence suite, with countermeasures launchers, missile approach warning sensors (MAWS) and RWR. Other stores options include the YJ-91A and YJ-12 supersonic anti-ship missiles as well as ECM pods. The version capable of launching the YJ-12 is sometimes known by the designation H-6L.

One of the original H-6 bombers being displayed in the central exhibition hall of the Military Museum, Beijing.

H-6M

The last of the H-6D derivatives to enter large-scale service is the H-6M for the PLAAF. This version appears to have been developed as an interim solution pending the arrival of the radically redesigned H-6K, and the first examples were probably produced via conversion of old H-6E/F airframes.

Xi'an H-6K

This H-6K is operated by the PLAAF's 108th Air Regiment, 36th Bomber Division, which has operated successive variants of the H-6 since the mid-1960s. The 108th Air Regiment flies both the H-6K and the H-6M from Wugong, Shaanxi Province.

47

BOMBERS & ATTACK AIRCRAFT

Xi'an H-6N

The H-6N includes an air-launched anti-ship ballistic missile, probably the CH-AS-X-13, a variant of the DF-21 anti-ship missile.

The H-6M has similarities with the naval H-6G, including the undernose radar and four underwing pylons. It also has an updated cockpit and self-defence improvements, including countermeasures launchers, MAWS, RWR and ECM pods. The H-6M entered PLAAF service in 2007 and is primarily armed with KD-20 and KD-63 cruise missiles.

H-6K: revamped version

In a surprise move, China unveiled a heavily reworked version of the 'Badger' in December 2006. This was the H-6K, also a specialist cruise missile carrier, but with an all-new forward fuselage featuring an airliner-style nose and a large radome. Enlarged engine air intakes are provided for the two Russian D-30KP-2 turbofans, another new feature, replacing the old WP-8/AM-3 turbojets. The new powerplant ensures longer range, higher cruising speed, larger payloads and greater efficiency.

In the cockpit, the H-6K boasts six colour multifunctional displays for the three-person crew as well as ejection seats. The aircraft features a forward-looking infra-red/TV turret below the nose, satellite communications, datalink antennas and comprehensive defensive aids, including MAWS and RWR. Most critically, the weapons system of the H-6K is based around KD-20 long-range cruise missiles, up to six of which can be carried under the wings. Older KD-63 missiles can also be used.

Current variants

A version of the H-6K for the PLAN is the H-6J, which entered service in late 2018 and is armed with up to six YJ-12 anti-ship missiles. More recently, it appears that at least some

CHINA'S 'BADGER' TANKERS

Versions of the H-6 have long served as the most important inflight refuelling tankers for the PLAAF and the PLAN. Development of Chinese 'Badger' tankers followed two discrete paths, with the H-6DU being produced via conversion of existing H-6D bombers. The H-6DU retains the original glazed nose and chin radome. Its mission equipment is made up of an RDC-1 hose-and-drogue refuelling pod installed under each wingtip.

The H-6DU is employed by the PLAN and is used primarily to support long-range fighter missions over the South China Sea and East China Sea. In contrast, the HU-6 is a dedicated tanker variant for the PLAAF, built as such from the outset. It has the nose glazing and chin radome deleted but is similarly equipped with a pair of RDC-1 refuelling pods.

BOMBERS & ATTACK AIRCRAFT

Xi'an H-6N

Weight (maximum take-off): 95,000kg (209,439lb)
Dimensions: Length 34.8m (114ft 2in), Wingspan 33m (108ft 3in), Height 10.36m (34ft)
Powerplant: Two Soloviev D-30KP-2 turbofan engines each rated at 118kN (27,000lb) thrust
Maximum speed: 1050km/h (650mph)
Range: 3500km (2200 miles)
Ceiling: 12,800m (42,000ft)
Crew: 4
Armament: Six underwing pylons for CH-AS-X-13 air-launched anti-ship ballistic missiles

The H-6K features enlarged engine inlets for the Soloviev D-30 turbofan engines, giving the aircraft a claimed combat radius of 3500 kilometres (2200 miles).

of these aircraft have been transferred to the PLAAF as part of a broader move to reallocate combat types to the air force. Finally, the H-6N version is another H-6K derivative, featuring an inflight refuelling probe and apparently dedicated to carrying anti-ship ballistic missiles (AShBMs). One of these enormous weapons, known to Western intelligence as the CH-AS-X-13, can be carried under the centreline. A handful of these aircraft are thought to be in service with the PLAAF, and they can alternatively be armed with KD-63 and KD-20 cruise missiles.

49

BOMBERS & ATTACK AIRCRAFT

Xi'an JH-7

Known by the Western reporting name 'Flounder' and named 'Flying Leopard' in China, the JH-7 is a twin-engine supersonic tactical strike and maritime attack aircraft, development of which began in the mid-1970s. However, its path to frontline service was a fairly tortuous one, hampered also by the differing requirements of the air force and navy.

Development of the JH-7 was originally prompted by Beijing's experiences in the Battle of the Paracel Islands, a 1974 conflict between the naval forces of China and South Vietnam.

In particular, the Chinese discovered that they had a serious lack of capable air support for maritime engagements of this kind.

Design proposals
In 1975, a request for proposals was issued to China's major aircraft design institutes calling for a strike aircraft that would be able to fulfil the requirements of both the PLAAF and the People's Liberation Army Navy – Naval Aviation. The fact that the two services had differing demands would make the development process more complicated. Namely, the PLAN wanted a tandem two-seat anti-shipping aircraft, while the PLAAF was looking for a heavy interdictor featuring side-by-side seating for its two crew.

Competing design proposals saw the development of the J-8 interceptor from Shenyang; the Nanchang Q-6, which was heavily inspired by the MiG-23; and a concept from Xi'an that was outwardly similar to the Anglo-French SEPECAT Jagua (although significantly larger).

Greenlit yet delayed
Eventually, Xi'an was authorized to proceed with its proposal, which was apparently judged less risky than the others, while still offering a good level of capability. However, in its early days, the programme was affected by the turmoil of the Cultural Revolution, and it was not until the 1980s that the domestic situation became more stable. At that point, however, there were no suitable engines available for what was initially known as the H-7.

Further compounding the issues was a proposal to split the H-7 into two discrete designs – one for the PLAAF and one for the PLAN. Finally, the decision was taken to pursue a

Xi'an JH-7A
Weight (maximum take-off): 28,475kg (62,777lb)
Dimensions: Length 22.32m (73ft 3in), Wingspan 12.8m (42ft), Height 6.22m (20ft 5in)
Powerplant: Two WS-9 turbofan engines each rated at 91.26kN (20,520lb) thrust with afterburning
Maximum speed: Mach 1.52
Range: around 1760km (1090 miles) with one inflight refuelling
Ceiling: 16,000m (52,000ft)
Crew: 2
Armament: One 23mm (0.9in) twin-barrel GSh-23 cannon plus a maximum of 9000kg (20,000lb) of disposable stores carried on nine hardpoints

BOMBERS & ATTACK AIRCRAFT

Xi'an JH-7
This JH-7A, serial number 73270, serves with the PLAAF's 126th Air Brigade, part of the Nanning Base, within Southern Theatre Command, and stationed at Liuzhou.

common design for both services, with the aircraft now being designated JH-7, in which the prefix stands for Jianjiji Hongzhaji or fighter-bomber.

With the indigenous WS-6 turbofan programme failing to produce the required powerplant, by the time the design of the JH-7 was finalized in 1983, it was decided instead to fit the aircraft with the British-supplied Rolls-Royce Spey 202. Ultimately, it was expected that the Spey would be superseded by a licence-produced version of the same engine known as the WS-9.

Prototypes and first flight
Six JH-7 prototypes were completed, and the first was rolled out in August 1988, taking to the air for the first time on 14 December 1988. Reflecting the troubled nature of the programme, it was not until 1998 that the JH-7 was finally officially approved for service after a very lengthy flight-test period.

Unfortunately, the protracted development phase and multiple problems encountered along the way led to the PLAAF losing interest in the JH-7 by the late 1990s. Instead, the air force began to look towards Russia to meet its combat aircraft requirements, and the Su-30MKK was chosen in preference to the Chinese design.

Beset by problems
However, the PLAN retained the JH-7 in its thinking and introduced the type as a dedicated maritime strike aircraft in 1994. At this stage, there were still various teething problems with the aircraft, especially regarding its all-important mission avionics, which were centred around the Type 232H multifunction fire-control radar. As a result, the first batch of around 18 aircraft was completed to an interim standard and introduced to service in an evaluation capacity.

Another lingering problem involved licenced production of the WS-9 engine, which forced Beijing to instead buy further examples of the Spey and delay the start of quantity production of the JH-7. Acquired in the early 2000s, this additional batch of Spey engines seemingly involved second-hand examples, since production had already ended by this time.

Once these additional engines had been secured, Xi'an was able to launch the manufacture of the JH-7 Block 02, which provided the first series-production version of the 'Flounder'. Other new features of the JH-7 Block 02 included a JL-10A multi-mode pulse-Doppler radar that offered improved performance in both air-to-ground and air-to-air modes. Once again, around 18 examples of the Block 02 aircraft appear to have been completed, and all were delivered to the PLAN.

Definitive engine
It was only in 2007 that the issues with the domestically produced engines were finally solved and the turbofan became available, now known under the WS-9 designation. Once the definitive engine had appeared, Xi'an was able to introduce a further improved version of the aircraft known as the JH-7A. The timing of this was fortuitous, since the PLAAF had concluded that buying yet more Su-30MKK strike aircraft from Russia was too expensive.

At the same time, the PLAAF still needed to replace obsolete H-5 light bombers and Q-5 attack aircraft, and the Su-30MKK was not able to use Chinese-made air-to-surface missiles, including the highly important YJ-8 cruise missile series.

BOMBERS & ATTACK AIRCRAFT

The JH-7 features two Xi'an WS-9 Qinling turbofan engines, allowing it to reach a maximum speed of 1808km/h (1123mph, 976kn).

With this in mind, the PLAAF chose to acquire the 'Flounder' too, now in its definitive JH-7A version. The design of the JH-7A had been finalized by early 2001, and the flight-test programme was launched in July 2002, when the first prototype of this version made its maiden flight.

JH-7A features

Compared to the JH-7, the JH-7A added a new digital cockpit with an updated head-up display as well as an inertial navigation system combined with GPS. Other avionics refinements brought a digital, dual-redundant fly-by-wire system that provided enhanced terrain-following capabilities. Externally, the JH-7A featured a modified wing with a revised planform and with the previous wing fences removed. The previous large ventral fin was also replaced by two smaller fins below the rear fuselage. Other less obvious external changes included a new one-piece windshield.

In terms of structure, the JH-7 also benefited from an increased use of composite materials, including the redesigned wing and tail. This served to reduce the overall weight of the airframe and provide for an increased fuel and weapons payload. For the carriage of its expanded range of weapons, the JH-7A's new wing was fitted with a pair of additional hardpoints, and two more pylons were also added below the engine air intakes to allow for the carriage of navigation/targeting pods. Weapons options included the YJ-83 air-to-surface missile and the YJ-91 anti-radiation

BOMBERS & ATTACK AIRCRAFT

missile, as well as laser-guided bombs and infrared-guided PL-8 air-to-air missiles for self-defence.

PLAN and PLAAF deliveries

Flight testing of the JH-7A version had been completed by early 2004, and in the middle of that year, the aircraft began to be delivered to operational units, starting with the PLAN. The PLAAF introduced the JH-7A to service around late 2004. As production continued for both services, the original batch of JH-7 aircraft appeared to have undergone modernization, bringing them up to a similar standard to the JH-7A in terms of avionics, including the new radar.

The JH-7A's long-range capability and two-person crew means that the aircraft lends itself to certain specialist missions, namely suppression of enemy air defences (SEAD). This led to the development of an electronic warfare version of the aircraft, which can carry a variety of different jamming or electronic intelligence (ELINT) pods. It appears that PLAAF tactics for the SEAD version involve the aircraft working in two-ship 'hunter-killer' teams, with one carrying pods to locate and/or jam hostile radio frequency emitters and the other being armed with Russian-made Kh-31P (AS-17 'Krypton') or Chinese YJ-91 anti-radiation missiles to target them.

Production of the JH-7A is thought to have ended around 2016. While the JH-7A is today being overshadowed by Russian- and Chinese-made multirole 'Flanker' derivatives, it remains a very useful long-range strike aircraft for the PLAAF, and has fulfilled an important maritime attack role for the PLAN.

The Xi'an JH-7A has a lighter and stronger airframe than the JH-7, allowing the newer aircraft to carry a maximum ordnance load of 9000kg (20,000lbs).

TRANSPORTS

Until relatively recently, the PLAAF's transport fleet was charged mainly with shorter-range movement of troops and cargo, primarily within China, as well as more general logistics and staff transport duties. As Beijing has taken on a more global role, its military has shifted its priorities toward force projection and out-of-area operations. Efforts to acquire strategic transport aircraft from Russia were generally difficult, spurring the development of the indigenous Y-20, which is arguably just as important to the PLAAF's future capabilities as the J-20 fighter.

- Nanchang Y-5
- Airbus A319
- Bombardier CRJ
- Ilyushin Il-76 and Il-78
- Xi'an Y-7
- Shaanxi Y-8
- Shaanxi Y-9
- Xi'an Y-20

A PLAAF Ilyushin Il-76MD military transport plane, serial number 21048, lands at Chkalovsky Air Force base in Russia, 2015.

TRANSPORTS

Nanchang Y-5

The classic Cold War-era Antonov An-2, which has the Western reporting name 'Colt', was widely exported by the Soviet Union, with China becoming one of the most enthusiastic operators of the biplane for both military and civilian purposes.

Beijing acquired a licence for the local production of the An-2, and the first Chinese-built example took to the air in 1957. Initially, production in China was handled by Nanchang. After several hundred examples had been completed, manufacture was transferred to Harbin in 1968. Most recently, the Y-5 has been built by the Shijiazhuang Aircraft Industry Company. The Chinese-built 'Colt' has enjoyed a remarkably long production run, with the thousandth example coming off the Shijiazhuang production line in late 1997. Limited production continued more recently, too.

China has made various improvements to the basic design, culminating in the Y-5B-200 version, which can be identified by the triple tipsails on the upper surfaces of the wings. Located close to the wingtips, these feather-like protrusions are said to improve the aircraft's rate of climb by 20 per cent as well as enhance the lift-to-drag ratio.

In PLAAF service, the Y-5 continues to be used in small numbers for training as well as liaison. In particular, the type is still appreciated as a robust and reliable platform for training paratroopers, being assigned to the Airborne Corps of the People's Liberation Army.

UAV version

Intriguingly, China has also developed an unmanned aerial vehicle version of the 'Colt', the Y-5U, which is based on the improved Y-5B airframe. This is apparently intended for short take-off and landing (STOL) cargo operations, especially in remote areas. The drone version of the Y-5 may well also have military applications.

Nanchang Y-5
Weight (maximum take-off): 5500kg (12,125lb)
Dimensions: Length 12.40m (40.7ft), Wingspan 18.20m (59.7ft), Height 4.10m (13.5ft)
Powerplant: One 750kW (1010hp) nine-cylinder Shvetsov ASh-62 radial engine
Maximum speed: 258km/h (160mph)
Range: 845km (525 miles)
Ceiling: 4500m (14,764ft)
Crew: 1–2

Students examine a Y-5 utility biplane during a visit to the Hebei Provincial Defense Technology School in Handan, Hebei province, 2018.

Airbus A319

The VIP transport arm of the PLAAF operates a combination of indigenous types and Western-produced airliners and helicopters. Among its fleet are three examples of the A319.

The A319 is a shorter-fuselage version of the popular A320 single-aisle jetliner. While based on commercial airliners, these aircraft are essentially private jets, although they offer a much greater range and cabin space than smaller business jets.

PLAAF usage

The PLAAF's aircraft are A319-115 Airbus Corporate Jets (ACJ), which were originally delivered to China United Airlines, being received in the airline's full livery. However, it seems that these aircraft were probably always destined for military service, and they were successively transferred to the PLAAF in September 2013, August 2014 and January 2015. Today, the VIP aircraft wear smart air force paint schemes complete with full PLAAF insignia.

Configuration

It is unclear exactly what configuration the PLAAF operates its A319s in, although a typical ACJ interior includes seating for up to 18 passengers, in a high degree of comfort. By way of comparison, the original airliner had seating for more than 130 passengers. In ACJ form, the A319's cabin is normally divided into separate VIP quarters, including an office, a bathroom with shower, sleeping quarters and a high-density passenger seating area.

100th Air Regiment

The operating unit is the 100th Air Regiment, part of the 34th Transport Division, and the aircraft are based at Beijing/Xijiao, in the Chinese capital. The aircraft – and other members of the air force VIP fleet – are directly assigned to the PLAAF Headquarters/Central Command.

Airbus A319-100
Airbus A319, registration B-4091, as seen at Beijing Xijiao Airport in August 2018, was first delivered to the PLAAF in 2014.

Airbus A319-100
Weight (maximum take-off): 78,000kg (171,961lb)
Dimensions: Length 33.84m (111ft), Wingspan 35.8m (117ft 5in), Height 11.76 m (38ft 7in)
Powerplant: Two 98–104.5kN (22,000 to 23,500lb) CFM56-5B7 or 5B7/P engines
Maximum speed: Mach 0.82 (871km/h; 541mph)
Range: 6945km (3750nm)
Ceiling: 11,900–12,500m (39,100–41,000ft)
Crew: 2; seating for 18 passengers
Capacity: 1550kg (3417lbs) cargo

TRANSPORTS

Bombardier CRJ

Several examples of the popular twin-engine Canadair Regional Jet (CRJ) series, produced by the Canadian Bombardier company, are operated by the 100th Air Regiment, which is the PLAAF's VIP transport arm.

These smaller business jets complement the larger, longer-range A319 and Boeing 737 and are used to move high-ranking personnel and government officials over shorter distances, primarily within China.

CRJ200ER

The PLAAF operates five CRJ200ER aircraft, which are also known as CL-600-2B19 Challenger 600s. These regional airliners wear the military serials B-4005, 4006, 4007, 4010 and 4011. All were introduced to service between September 1997 and June 1988. While the basic CRJ200ER can seat up to 50 passengers, the Corporate Jetliner version, optimised for executive use, has seating for 18–30 passengers.

CRJ700/CRJ200

The Chinese military also flies a dozen examples of the CRJ700, also known as CL-600-2C10 Challenger 870s. These comprise a mix of standard CRJ700s and extended-range CRJ700ER versions. The military serials for these aircraft comprise B-4060, 4061, 4062, 4063, 4064, 4065, 4067, 4068, 4069, 4661 and 4662. These aircraft were

Bombardier CL-600-2B19 Challenger 600
This PLAAF Bombardier Challenger 600, registration B-4005, was seen at Beijing Xijiao Airport in May 2022.

acquired between January 2005 and February 2015 and at least one is believed to be assigned to the People's Liberation Army Navy (PLAN).

A stretched derivative of the CRJ200, the CRJ700 offers seating for a maximum of 78 passengers in its regional airliner version, although the configuration used by the PLAAF is unclear. Additionally, the CRJ700 features new wings with leading-edge slats and a slightly widened fuselage with a lowered floor.

Bombardier CL-600-2C10 Challenger 870
This Bombardier Challenger 870, registration B-4067, was first delivered to the PLAAF in September 2014.

TRANSPORTS

Bombardier CL-600-2B19 Challenger 600
This People's Liberation Army Naval Air Force (PLANAF) Bombardier Challenger 600, registration B-4701, was seen at Shanghai Pudong Airport in July 2022.

Bombadier Challenger 600
Weight (maximum take-off): 23,133kg (51,000lb)
Dimensions: Length 26.77m (87ft 10in), Wingspan 21.21m (69ft 7in), Height 6.22m (20ft 5in)
Powerplant: Two General Electric CF34-3B1 turbofan engines, 38.84kN (8,730lbf) thrust each
Cruise speed: 819km/h (509mph)
Range: 5,206km (3,235 mi, 2,811 nmi)
Ceiling: 12,500m (41,000ft)
Crew: 2 + 1; seating for 18–30 passengers

Bombadier Challenger 870
Weight (maximum take-off): 24,040kg (53,000lb)
Dimensions: Length 32.3m (106ft), Wingspan 23.2m (76ft 3in), Height 7.6m (24ft 10in)
Powerplant: Two GE CF34-8C5B1 turbofan engines, 38.84kN (8,730lbf) thrust each
Cruise speed: 876km/h (544mph)
Range: 5,206km (3,235 mi, 2,811 nmi)
Ceiling: 12,500m (41,000ft)
Crew: 2 + 1; seating for 18–30 passengers

Bombardier CL-600-2C10 Challenger 870
This PLANAF Bombardier Challenger 870, registration B-4661, was seen in an undisclosed location in July 2023.

TRANSPORTS

Ilyushin Il-76 and Il-78

First flown in March 1971, the Il-76 was the Soviet Union's primary strategic airlifter. Until the arrival of the Y-20, the Il-76 was also the PLAAF's most important heavy-lift military transport, but acquiring it – and the Il-78 'Midas' aerial refuelling tanker version – would prove a major challenge for Beijing.

The first Il-76s (Western reporting name 'Candid') for the PLAAF were acquired via the Civil Aviation Administration of China (CAAC), which secured a total of 14 between 1991 and 1996. These arrived in China in two batches supplied by the factory named after Valery Chkalov in Tashkent, Uzbekistan. It seems a major portion of these aircraft were unarmed Il-76TD versions with the rear gun and other military equipment removed. Later, the military-standard Il-76MD was also supplied.

Chinese usage

The first Chinese 'Candids' entered service with China United Airlines, wearing civilian markings, before being transferred to the PLAAF's 13th Transport Division. The Il-76s were initially used primarily in support of China's airborne forces. In this role, the Il-76MD can carry up to 126 paratroopers, who are parachuted via the rear hatch as well as via doors on each side of the fuselage. As well as troops, the aircraft can airdrop cargoes, including vehicles, such as three of the PLA's ZBD-03 airborne infantry fighting vehicles. Military equipment can be dropped from high altitudes or from an altitude of just 3–5m (10–16ft) above the ground, with the cargo extracted using a small parachute.

The combination of the Il-76's long range and useful cargo capacity – 7400km (4598 miles) with a payload of 20,000kg (44,092lb) – amounted to a quantum leap in the PLA's ability to rapidly project power far beyond China's borders. While the PLAAF clearly valued its Il-76s, it had to give up four examples for conversion as KJ-2000 airborne early warning and control (AEW&C) aircraft.

Deal with Russia

In the mid-2000s, it appears that Beijing agreed a deal with Russia's Rosoboronexport arms export agency, which would have seen it acquire 34 more Il-76MDs and four Il-78 tankers. However, for various reasons, this never came to fruition. It is likely that the end of Il-76 production in Tashkent and the subsequent relocation of the manufacturing effort to Russia was a major factor.

As an alternative, China began to scour the market for second-hand Il-76s. In 2012, China received three more Il-76s that were overhauled in Russia prior to delivery. Among them

---

Ilyushin Il-76MD
Weight (maximum take-off): 190,000kg (418,878lb)
Dimensions: Length 46.59m (152ft 10in), Wingspan 50.5m (165ft 8in), Height 14.76m (48ft 5in)
Powerplant: Four Aviadvigatel/Perm D-30KP series 2 (izdeliye 53) turbofans, each rated at 117.68kN (26,455lbf)
Maximum speed: 750-780km/h (466-485mph)
Range: 7400km (4598 miles)
Ceiling: 12,000m (39,370ft)
Crew: 5
Capacity: 20,000kg (44,092lb) cargo

Ilyushin Il-76MD
This PLAAF Ilyushin Il-76MD, registration B-4039, was first seen at Macau International Airport in 2007, the first sighting of the type in Chinese service.

TRANSPORTS

Ilyushin Il-76MD
This PLAAF Ilyushin Il-76MD, registration 21045, was seen at Zhuhai Jinwan Airport in October 2021.

was at least one Il-76TD. In 2013, another contract was announced, by Rosoboronexport this time, covering 12 refurbished Il-76MD aircraft.

Just as important as the PLAAF's long-range transport capabilities is its fleet of aerial refuelling tankers. The demand for new tanker capacity was driven to a significant degree by the fact that the PLAAF's Su-30MKK fighters were not compatible with the existing HU-6 tankers.

China turned again to the second-hand market in a bid to acquire the Il-78, the tanker version of the Il-76. In 2011, it was reported that a contract had been signed with Ukraine, which had inherited several Il-78s from former Soviet military stocks. The deal appears to have covered three aircraft, which were refurbished in Ukraine before being delivered to the PLAAF. The first example was noted in China in 2014, and two more were delivered to the PLAAF's 13th Division in 2015 and 2016.

Ilyushin Il-78
As far as is known, only three Il-78s were ever supplied to China, with current efforts instead focused on a tanker version of the Y-20 transport. The Il-78 is equipped with three UPAZ-1A refuelling pods, one under each wing and one on the left side of the rear fuselage. The PLAAF's Il-78s are regularly used to support Su-30MKKs on long-range patrol missions over the East China Sea and the South China Sea.

Ilyushin Il-78
Weight (maximum take-off): 210,000kg (462,971lb)
Dimensions: Length 46.59m (152ft 10in), Wingspan 50.5m (165ft 8in), Height 14.76m (48ft 5in)
Powerplant: Four Aviadvigatel/Perm D-30KP series 2 (izdeliye 53) turbofans, each rated at 117.68kN (26,455lbf)
Maximum speed: 850km/h (530mph)
Range: 7300km (4,500 miles)
Ceiling: 12,000m (39,370ft)
Crew: 6
Capacity: 48,000 (105,822lb) cargo

Ilyushin Il-78
This PLAAF Ilyushin Il-78, registration 20641, was seen in an undisclosed location in January 2021.

TRANSPORTS

Xi'an Y-7

Another aviation product of the Soviet Union that has been licence-built in China was the Antonov An-24 turboprop regional transport, produced by Xi'an as the Y-7 in a number of successively improved versions and manufactured for export as the MA-60.

Xi'an Y-7-100
This PLAAF Xi'an Y-7-100, registration 55110, is shown as seen at Beijing Shahezhen Air Base in July 2020.

Xi'an began work on the Y-7 in the mid-1960s, and the first example of this aircraft – actually a Chinese-assembled An-24T cargo transport – flew on 25 December 1970. The upheavals of the Cultural Revolution in China meant that large-scale production of the Y-7 did not commence until around 1982. The first aircraft for the PLAAF began to be delivered in around 1984.

Y-7-100 development
Work on an improved version, the Y-7-100, was launched in the mid-1980s, and this emerged essentially as an unlicenced variant of the An-26. Therefore, it features a fully pressurized fuselage, a rear cargo ramp, more powerful WJ-5E turboprop engines, an auxiliary turbojet and a modernized cockpit. The aircraft also features characteristic wingtip winglets.

In PLAAF service, this variant is known to the factory as the Y-7H-500 and to the military as the Y-7H. First

Xi'an Y-7-100
Weight (maximum take-off): 21,800kg (48,061lb)
Dimensions: Length 24.2m (79ft 5in), Wingspan 29.67m (97ft 3in), Height 8.6m (28ft 2in)
Powerplant: Two Dongan WJ-5E turboprop engines, 1800kW (2400shp) each equivalent
Maximum speed: 505km/h (314mph)
Range: 910km ((565 miles)
Ceiling: 8750m (28,707ft)
Crew: 3; plus 52 passengers

flown in 1989, it is used primarily as a tactical transport.

Y-7G export model
Developed for export, the MA-60 is based on the Y-7 but has a new stretched fuselage with seating for up to 60 passengers. This aircraft made its first flight in 2000 and subsequently entered PLAAF service as the Y-7G. Its missions include VIP transport and search and rescue, while the People's Liberation Army Navy also employs it for shuttle flights to Chinese-controlled islands in the South China Sea.

TRANSPORTS

Xi'an Y-7G

A PLAAF Xi'an Y-7G, registration 55017, dating from February 2022.

Xi'an Y-7G

Weight (maximum take-off): 21,800kg (48,061lb)
Dimensions: Length 24.7m (81ft 1in), Wingspan 29.2m (95ft 10in), Height 8.86m (29ft 1in)
Powerplant: Two Pratt & Whitney Canada PW127J turbo prop engines, 2051kW (2750hp) each
Maximum speed: 514km/h (319mph)
Range: 1600km (990 mi, 860 nmi)
Ceiling: 7620m (25,000ft)
Crew: 3; plus 60 passengers

HYJ-7 BOMBER TRAINER

A unique version of the Y-7 employed by the PLAAF is the HYJ-7 (also designated Y-7LH), a training aircraft based on the Y-7-100C2 passenger transport. Introduced in the late 1990s, the aircraft is used to train navigators and bombardiers destined to operate the H-6 bomber. Changes compared to the transport version include a large observation gondola on the starboard side of the fuselage with glazing to represent the nose of the H-6. Equipment includes a bombsight, a bomb computer and a new navigation system. Long fairings on each side of the lower fuselage carry up to 20 small practice bombs. To represent more modern versions of the H-6, it appears that some aircraft have also received an attack radar and datalink antennas. The HYJ-7 is also in service with the navy.

Xi'an Y-7G

This Chinese Navy (PLANAF) Xi'an Y-7G, registration 9082, was photographed in Changchun Longjia International Airport in July 2022.

TRANSPORTS

Shaanxi Y-8

The Soviet-designed Antonov An-12 (Western reporting name 'Cub') was the pre-eminent Eastern Bloc four-engine tactical transport during the Cold War. China embarked on domestic development of the aircraft as the Shaanxi Y-8, which has had an illustrious career.

While other projects to licence-build Soviet aircraft designs – especially for fighters – faltered under the pressure of the Sino-Soviet split beginning in the early 1960s, the Y-8 fared much better. In the same decade, China acquired a small number of An-12s from the Soviet Union and embarked on an indigenous production effort. This yielded tangible results when the first example assembled using Soviet-produced components took to the air in December 1974.

First flight

Initially, the Y-8 programme was handled by Xi'an, but it was turned over to Shaanxi soon after the aircraft's first flight. Here, the programme also changed from being one of licenced production to one characterized by reverse engineering. The first Shaanxi-built Y-8 made its maiden flight in December 1975, with serial production being launched in 1981.

The reverse engineering process resulted in some changes compared with the An-12. The glazed nose of the Y-8 is longer, while the tail turret is derived from that used in the H-6 bomber; the twin 23mm (0.9in) guns were soon deleted entirely. For moving cargo loads, the Y-8 features a roller-type system, replacing the conveyor belt type used on the Soviet aircraft.

Load specs

The basic Y-8 transport can carry up to 20,000kg (44,092lb) of cargo. Alternative loads include up to 96 soldiers or 82 paratroopers in the main cargo compartment. The aircraft can also be configured for medical evacuation (medevac), in which capacity it can carry 60 soldier casualties on stretchers, or 20 walking wounded plus three medical attendants.

The initial production batch was made up of Y-8 aircraft, with the first

Shaanxi Y-8C
Weight (maximum take-off): 61,000kg (134,100lbs)
Dimensions: Length 34m (111ft 6in), Wingspan 38m (124ft 7in), Height 11.16m (36ft 7in)
Powerplant: Four Zhuzhou WoJiang WJ-6 turboprops, developing 3170kW (4250hp)
Maximum speed: 660km/h (410mph)
Range: 5615km (3489 miles)
Ceiling: 10,400m (34,120ft)
Crew: 5
Capacity: 20,000kg (44,092lb); 96 troops or 82 paratroops; or up to 60 medevac patients
Armament: Two 23mm (0.9in) cannon

Shaanxi Y-8C
This Y-8C (serial number 55415), the basic transport version of the type, was seen in Zhengzhou International Airport, China, in April 2023.

TRANSPORTS

Shaanxi Y-8F-100
This Y-8F-100 (serial number B-4155), seen in Hanzhong, China, in June 2023, is fitted with an electronic flight instrument system (EFIS), colour weather radar, traffic collision avoidance system (TCAS) and GPS.

major sub-variant for the PLAAF being the Y-8A. This was reportedly developed specifically to transport US-supplied S-70C Black Hawk helicopters into Tibet. Key changes included a rear loading ramp to allow easier access for helicopter cargoes.

Y-8C

The early versions of the Y-8 – also known as the Category I Platform – were hampered by a lack of pressurization in the cargo hold. This meant they could only operate at higher altitudes with a maximum of 14 passengers, who were provided with a pressurized crew cabin in the forward part of the fuselage. A version with a fully pressurized cargo hold was developed as the Y-8C, which made its maiden flight in December 1990. This revised aircraft is also designated as the Category II Platform.

Other changes in the Y-8C include a simplified rear loading ramp – a one-piece unit compared to the previous two-piece cargo doors that opened inwards.

The Y-8C became the most widespread version of the 'Cub' in PLAAF service and spawned some specialized derivatives, including the Y-8H for aerial survey. Other Y-8Cs have been adapted as avionics testbeds, including, for example, being fitted with the radome and the indigenously developed radar of the J-11B fighter.

Y-8E

A more unusual development was the Y-8E, a dedicated drone carrier that replaced the Tu-4 previously used in this role. Work began in the late 1980s and the aircraft apparently entered small-scale service in around 1990. The Y-8E can carry a WZ-5 drone under each wing, which can be launched in mid-air and then recovered by parachute after completing its mission. Additional equipment includes a new mission computer, inertial navigation system/GPS and TV and infrared cameras.

Interestingly, China developed its WZ-5 drones based on examples of

Shaanxi Y-8F-100

Weight (maximum take-off): 61,000kg (134,100lbs)
Dimensions: Length 34m (111ft 6in), Wingspan 38m (124ft 7in), Height 11.16m (36ft 7in)
Powerplant: Four Zhuzhou WoJiang WJ-6 turboprops, each developing 3126kW (4192.035hp)
Maximum speed: 660km/h (410mph)
Range: 5615km (3489 miles)
Ceiling: 10,400m (34,120ft)
Crew: 5
Capacity: 96 troops or 82 paratroops; or up to 60 medevac patients
Armament: Two 23mm (0.9in) cannon

TRANSPORTS

People's Liberation Army (PLA) paratroopers jump from a Chinese Y-8 aircraft during a two week-long Pakistan-China military exercise in Jhelum, Pakistan, November 2011. PLA soldiers and Pakistani commandos participated in the combined exercise, in a display designed to bolster ties between the two countries.

the US-made AQM-34N Firebee high-altitude reconnaissance UAV, several of which had been shot down over Chinese territory during the 1960s.

Y-8F-400

A programme to develop a 'second-generation' Y-8 resulted in the Y-8F-400. This aircraft has enhanced avionics and a flight crew of three, compared with five on earlier aircraft. The glazed nose is replaced by a solid nose and the fully pressurized cargo hold adds an overhead cargo conveyor in addition to the rollers in the floor.

However, the Y-8F-400 did not enter PLAAF service as a transport, instead providing the basis for a wide range of special mission aircraft (see Chapter 4).

Shaanxi Y-9

In the early 2000s, China set about developing a reworked version of its Y-8 four-engine tactical transport to create an aircraft much better suited to the requirements of the PLAAF in the 21st century. The result was the Y-9 (Western reporting name: 'Claw').

The modernization effort that finally led to the Y-9 reportedly involved Antonov – the Ukrainian design bureau responsible for the original An-12. The scale of the overhaul was far more than just cosmetic. In terms of the airframe, the wing and the fuselage were subject to a redesign. Other improvements include small vertical stabilizers mounted on the horizontal tailplanes, likely to improve stability at low speeds. The aircraft is reportedly able to carry almost twice as much fuel as the Y-8 for a considerable improvement in range.

Early development
As well as Antonov, engine supplier Pratt & Whitney Canada (P&WC) was also involved in the development of the new-generation airlifter, which was originally known as the Y-8F600 or, alternatively, the Category III Platform. Other Western companies also contributed at this early stage, especially in terms of the aircraft's modern avionics. Development was reportedly launched in 1999, with Antonov and P&WC having joined the programme by the early 2000s.

While the Y-8F600 was, officially at least, a civilian product for commercial use, it was very rapidly militarized as the Y-9. The Y-9 also includes a much greater degree of indigenous equipment, including WJ-6C turboprops driving new six-blade composite propellers. The Chinese content in the Y-9 circumvents restrictions on Western engines and avionics for military applications.

First flight
The Y-9/Category III Platform prototype completed its maiden flight on 14 January 2005. Interestingly, the airlifter appears to have become known in the West only after the appearance of the Y-8GX-6, an anti-submarine warfare

Shaanxi Y-9
Serial number 10255 is operated by the 4th Division's 10th Air Regiment, within the Western Theatre Command. The unit's new-generation Y-9s serve alongside Y-8Cs based at Chengdu-Qionglai air base.

Shaanxi Y-9
Weight (maximum take-off): 265,352kg (585,000lb)
Dimensions: Length 36.07m (118ft 4in), Wingspan 38m (124ft 8in), Height 11.3m (37ft 1in)
Powerplant: Four WoJiang WJ-6C turboprop engines each rated at 3805kW (5103hp)
Maximum speed: 650km/h (400mph)
Range: 2200km (1400 miles) with 15,000kg (33,069lb) payload
Ceiling: 10,400m (34,100ft)
Crew: 4
Capacity: 98 paratroopers, 72 medevac patients or 20,000kg (44,092lb) of cargo

aircraft based on the same airframe. Initially, and somewhat confusingly, special-mission variants based on the Y-9/Category III Platform airframe retained designations in the Y-8 series.

The Y-9 airlifter offers a range of advantages over its Y-8 predecessor, not only in terms of improved performance and modern avionics. The cargo hold is also longer, and while the aircraft can transport loads of up to 20,000kg (44,092lb), these can be larger dimensionally, including military vehicles, helicopters and cargo containers. The aircraft can also reportedly now carry 98 paratroopers compared to 82 in the Y-8. Loads of up to 13,200kg (29,101lb) can be airdropped via the rear ramp. Paratroopers are delivered both from the rear ramp and doors on the sides of the fuselage. In medical evacuation (medevac) configuration, the Y-9 can transport 72 stretcher patients plus three medical attendants, or 98 walking wounded. The flight deck is equipped for operations by a flight crew of four. These are provided with six colour multifunction displays, with an electronic flight instrument system (EFIS) to display primary flight data. The new solid nose of the Y-9 (in contrast to the glazing of the Y-8) covers a navigation radar, and the aircraft also features an advanced communication suite. Collision avoidance systems are also included for safer operations, especially in poor weather.

Y-9 PLAAF service

The greater demand for special-missions versions based on the Y-9/Category III Platform meant that the transport version of the Y-9 only appeared in PLAAF service somewhat later. At one stage, it was even suggested that the Y-9 transport might be abandoned in favour of continued production of the Y-8C.

Finally, a true prototype of the Y-9 took to the air in November 2010, with series production launched soon after and service entry with the PLAAF commencing in 2012.

A Y-9 transport aircraft performs during Airshow China 2021 in Zhuhai, Guangdong Province, China.

HARBIN Y-12

Understood to have the Western reporting name 'Chan', the Y-12 is a light utility transport with short take-off and landing (STOL) capabilities.

Development of the Y-12 began sometime in the late 1970s, the aircraft being based on the previous Harbin Y-11, of which around 50 examples were completed for civilian service in China. Compared to the Y-11, the Y-12 introduced several enhancements, including a redesigned wing and a larger fuselage. The Y-12 took to the air in 1980 but was soon superseded by the Y-12II, first flown in 1984, with various improvements, including more powerful engines.

Later military versions of the Y-12 are powered by indigenous engines, which replace the standard Pratt & Whitney Canada (P&WC) PT6A turboprops. From the Y-12IV onwards, therefore, the aircraft was fitted with indigenous WJ-9 engines.

MAIN VERSIONS

Primary PLAAF versions of the aircraft include the Y-12C, the military version of the Y-12IV, which is used for aerial survey and paratrooper training. The improved Y-12D reportedly entered PLAAF service in 2015 and is primarily used by the 15th Airborne Corps for paratrooper training. It has improved WJ-9 engines and military avionics, including radios, inertial navigation system/GPS and a forward-looking infrared (FLIR) sensor. It can carry around 10 paratroopers.

The ultimate military version is the Y-12F, which appeared in late 2010 with more powerful P&WC engines and a redesigned airframe, including new wings and fuselage. The Y-12F has a greater payload and range than its predecessors and first entered service with the paramilitary China Marine Surveillance (CMS) service. Other examples of the Y-12 are operated by the China Coast Guard.

Xi'an Y-20

While the Y-20 has not been overshadowed by its new-generation near-contemporary, the J-20 stealth fighter, the four-engine long-range transport is arguably just as important in terms of the modernization of the PLAAF and especially to Beijing's wider strategic ambitions.

In China, the Y-20 is officially known as the Kunpeng – named after a giant mythical bird similar to the roc – befitting its status as the country's largest indigenous aircraft type.

Development of the Y-20 was launched at Xi'an in the early 2000s, with the design work being handled by that company's No. 603 Institute. Also involved in the project were Chengdu and Shenyang as subcontractors, while the Ukrainian Antonov Bureau apparently had a role during the design phase. The exact degree

Xi'an Y-20

An early-production Y-20, serial number 11057 is on strength with the 12th Air Regiment of the 4th Division. The aircraft is based at Chengdu-Qionglai.

TRANSPORTS

of involvement that the Ukrainian company had in the Y-20 project remains unclear, however.

The need for a new strategic transport was increased by Beijing's problems in securing enough Soviet-era Il-76 airlifters for the PLAAF. While two small batches were acquired in the early 1990s, a larger order in the mid-2000s fell through, as you can read about in the separate entry on the Il-76/Il-78. As a stopgap measure, China did manage to secure some additional second-hand Il-76s. Meanwhile, work on the Y-20 programme was accelerated.

First flight and flight tests

The first prototype Y-20 was completed sometime between 2009 and 2012 and following taxi tests in late 2012 made its maiden flight on 26 January 2013. By the end of the same year, another two examples had been produced, one of them for static tests, and two more prototypes followed in 2015. Flight tests were completed at various different locations, including at very high altitude, to ensure that the aircraft met the full spectrum of PLAAF requirements.

The Y-20 is frequently compared to both the Il-76 and the US-designed C-17 Globemaster III. Based on its payload attributes, the Y-20 is smaller than the C-17 and much closer to the Il-76. However, even though it is somewhat shorter than the Il-76 overall, it features a wider and taller cargo compartment than the Soviet

Xi'an Y-20A

Weight (maximum take-off): 180,000kg (396,832lb)
Dimensions: Length 47m (154ft 2in), Wingspan 50m (164ft 1in)
Powerplant: Four Soloviev D-30KP-2 turbofan engines, each rated at 117.68kN (26,460lb)
Maximum speed: Mach 0.75
Range: 7800km (4800 miles) with payload of two main battle tanks
Ceiling: 13,000m (43,000ft)
Crew: 3
Capacity: 300 troops, 110 paratroopers, 200 medevac patients or equivalent cargo load

A PLAAF Xi'an Y-20 is shown here during a diplomatic visit at Sheremetyevo International Airport, Russia, 2020.

design. This allows a greater variety of larger items to be carried, including main battle tanks. In fact, there are suggestions that the entire design may have been reworked at an early stage to ensure that modern tanks like the 58 ton (52.6 tonne) Type 99A2 could be accommodated.

Modern wing design

The Y-20 has a broadly similar wingspan to the Il-76 but the wing itself is of a much more modern design, with high-lift devices and an efficient supercritical aerofoil section. Combined with a higher aspect ratio and reduced sweep on the trailing edge, the Y-20's wing contributes to a greater range than that achieved by the Il-76. The high-lift devices on the leading and trailing edges of the wing, together with a heavy-duty undercarriage with six pairs of mainwheels, help improve short-field performance, an attribute also shared with the C-17.

Features and specifications

Looking at the Y-20 in detail, the aircraft has a conventional overall layout for a heavy military transport. However, it makes extensive use of composite materials in its construction, helping to reduce overall airframe weight. The Y-20 is also equipped with modern avionics from the outset, with a digital flight deck for the flight crew of three. Avionics otherwise include a digital fly-by-wire flight control system, satellite communications and a small forward-looking infrared (FLIR) sensor for take-off and landing in poor weather conditions.

Like certain other Chinese aircraft designs, the Y-20 was initially hamstrung by the relatively poor performance of its engines. These Russian-supplied D-30KP-2s, which are low-bypass units, do not produce the same level of thrust as more modern high-bypass powerplants of equivalent size. Ultimately, however, Xi'an planned to re-engine the Y-20 with a higher-thrust domestically produced powerplant, the high-bypass WS-20. A deal was secured with Moscow for the supply of D-30KP-2s, with reports of an initial batch of 55 to be delivered by 2012. In 2011, it appears that a follow-on order was placed for 184 more D-30-series engines, to power both the Y-20 as well as the H-6K bomber and its derivatives.

The WS-20, meanwhile, is apparently based on the core of the military WS-10A turbofan as used in the J-11B and J-16 fighters. It was tested inflight onboard an Il-76 testbed before being introduced on the Y-20B version. In late 2015, it was officially announced that testing of the Y-20 was completed and that serial production had been launched. The first aircraft handover to the PLAAF took place in June 2016, after which the aircraft was officially introduced to PLAAF service as the Y-20A.

Active service

The initial operating unit was the 4th Transport Division's 12th Air Regiment based at Qionglai, near Chengdu. After first breaking cover in late 2020, additional imagery of the re-engined Y-20B version began to circulate in early 2023, with reports from China claiming that it had now also entered PLAAF service, although likely only on a trial basis.

Overall, the Y-20 is set to play a very important role in helping the Chinese military meet its wider ambitions, including deploying and sustaining forces over much greater distances. The same basic airframe has also been further developed as an inflight refuelling tanker, with rumours that an airborne early warning and control (AEW&C) derivative may also be planned.

YY-20 TANKER VERSION

The demands for new and additional tanker capacity spurred the development of an inflight refuelling version of the Y-20, with the initial YY-20A being based on the Y-20A airframe with the Russian-made D-30KP-2 engines.

First noted in a satellite image from late 2018, the YY-20A tanker is fitted with a hose-and-drogue refuelling pod under each wing, while a third centreline refuelling station is installed below the rear fuselage, primarily for topping up larger aircraft.

Other changes include infrared and TV optical devices to help coordinate with the aircraft being refuelled. With the internal fuel tank removed from the cargo hold, the YY-20A can also be used as transport.

In mid-2021, imagery appeared suggesting the YY-20A was in service with the PLAAF. By the end of that year, evidence had also emerged of a re-engined version, likely designated YY-20B, with the definitive WS-20 engines now installed. The improved performance of these powerplants also likely results in an increased payload of fuel being available for transfer.

SPECIAL MISSION AIRCRAFT

China operates a uniquely diverse fleet of special mission aircraft, fulfilling a wide variety of roles, including airborne early warning and control, electronic and signals intelligence (ELINT and SIGINT), airborne command post, offensive electronic countermeasures (ECM), as well as anti-submarine and psychological warfare. The backbone of this fleet is provided by adaptations of the venerable Shaanxi Y-8 transport, as well as its more advanced successor, the Y-9. Other such platforms are based on transport aircraft of both Soviet and Western origin.

- Antonov An-30
- Boeing 737
- Learjet Model 35 and Model 36
- Tupolev Tu-154
- Shaanxi KJ-200
- Shaanxi KJ-500
- Xi'an KJ-2000
- Shaanxi Y-8 & Y-9 Special Missions Versions

A Shaanxi KJ-500A airborne early warning and control (AEW&C) aircraft arrives at Zhuhai Air Show Center on 3 November 2022.

SPECIAL MISSION AIRCRAFT

Antonov An-30

Developed in the Soviet Union, the An-30 (Western reporting name 'Clank') was built by Antonov in Kyiv but was designed by Beriev in Taganrog. Today it remains in only limited PLAAF service.

Derived from the An-24 transport – which China built locally as the Y-7 – the An-30 is a dedicated aerial survey platform. The An-30 was first flown on 21 August 1967, at which time it was still known as the An-24FK (Foto-Kartografichesky).

Equipment and setup
Compared to the An-24 transport, the An-30 features a revised forward fuselage with a raised cockpit for the two pilots plus a glazed navigator's compartment. A flight engineer and communications operator are also carried. In terms of equipment, the An-30 carries an array of optical cameras for photo-survey. There is provision for four cameras inside the cabin: two for oblique photography and two for vertical photography. These take photos via a series of hatches in the cabin floor. A small dark room is also provided for film reloading.

It is unclear which version of the An-30 China acquired, although the main derivatives were the An-30A for civilian use, the An-30B for military customers (with a different navigation system and more camera options) and the long-range An-30D.

PLAAF service
In PLAAF service, the few remaining An-30s are apparently now operated by an Independent (Aerial Survey) Regiment based at Hanzhong-Chenggu in Shaanxi province. Previously, these aircraft were assigned to the 106th Aerial Survey Regiment, 36th Bomber Division, at the same base. The unit also flies the Y-8H1 and Y-12-IV, both also equipped for photo survey.

SPECIAL MISSION AIRCRAFT

Antonov An-30

PLAAF An-30, serial number 1001, registration 873, seen off airport in March 2023.

Antonov An-30

Weight (maximum take-off): 23,000kg (50,706lb)
Dimensions: Length: 24.26m (79ft 7in), Wingspan: 29.19m (95ft 9in), Height: 8.32m (27ft 3.5in)
Powerplant: Two Ivchenko Progress AI-24VT turbo-props, each rated at 2103kW (2820hp), and one Soyuz RU-19A-300 turbojet rated at 900kg (1984lb) of thrust
Maximum speed: 540km/h (336mph)
Range: 2630km (1634 miles) with maximum fuel
Ceiling: 8300m (27,230ft)
Crew: 5

Antonov An-30

A PLAAF An-30, serial number 1507, registration 3710, seen in 2017.

SPECIAL MISSION AIRCRAFT

Boeing 737

The ubiquitous Boeing 737 is one of the more unlikely aircraft in Chinese military service. The classic twinjet is used in two distinct roles by the PLAAF: as an airborne command post and as a VIP transport.

The PLAAF appears to have obtained a total of 14 Boeing 737s in three different variants. These are made up of eight 737-3Q8s (serials B-4008, B-4009, B-4018 to B-4021, B-4052 and B-4053), two 737-76Ds (B-4025 and B-4026) and four 737-85Ns (B-4080 to B-4083). Initially, it appears that the entire 737 fleet was assigned to the 34th Transport Division for use as VIP transports.

The aircraft were originally operated in a civilian-style China United Airlines paint scheme. This later gave way, at least on some of the aircraft, to full PLAAF insignia.

Airborne command posts

The arrival of the Airbus A319 in the VIP role may well have freed up two 737-3Q8s for other duties. Regardless, B-4052 and B-4053 were both converted to become airborne command posts. Beijing did this without US approval, the aircraft having originally been purchased by China United Airlines in 1990 and later serving as VIP transports with the PLAAF.

Boeing 737-300
PLAAF Boeing 737 (registration B-4021) at Poznan Lawica Airport, Poland, in July 2013. The aircraft was first delivered in September 1995.

SPECIAL MISSION AIRCRAFT

Boeing 737-300
First delivered in 2000, this Boeing 737-300, serial number B-4052, was converted by Xi'an into an airborne command post for the PLAAF, and allocated to the 102nd Air Regiment at Beijing/Nanyuan.

Boeing 737-300
Weight (maximum take-off): 56,740kg (124,500lb)
Dimensions: Length: 33.40m (109ft 7in), Wingspan: 28.88m (94ft 9in), Height: 11.13m (36ft 6in)
Powerplant: Two 89.0kN (20,000lb) CFM International CFM563B1 turbofans, or optionally two 97.9kN (22,000lb) CFM563B2
Cruising speed: 908km/h (564mph)
Range: 4973km (2685nm)
Ceiling: 11,300m (37,000ft)
Crew: 2; plus 110 passengers first class configuration

Boeing 737-800
At least four 737-800s were delivered to the PLAAF, at first to be used as VIP transports.

Conversion upgrade
Work to transform the two 737s as airborne command posts was reportedly conducted by Xi'an. The aircraft received a prominent fairing on top of the forward fuselage and two smaller fairings below the mid-section of the fuselage. These almost certainly house satellite communications and datalink antennas.

Immediately after modification, these two 737s were painted light grey. They were later changed to a scheme closer to that found on the PLAAF's VIP transport fleet. While the VIP 737s are assigned to the 34th Transport Division's 100th Air Regiment based at Beijing/Xijiao, the airborne command posts are apparently flown by the 102nd Air Regiment at Beijing/Nanyuan.

SPECIAL MISSION AIRCRAFT

Learjet Model 35 and Model 36

The PLAAF's long-serving but little-known small fleet of Learjet 35 and 36 business jets initially served in a special-missions role, although it is possible that, in more recent years, at least some may have switched to more routine staff transport and liaison duties.

According to the Stockholm International Peace Research Institute (SIPRI), which tracks global arms sales, China acquired the Learjets in 1985-86 'for geographical survey'. The aircraft comprised three Learjet 35As (serials B-4186 to B-4188) and two Learjet 36As (serials B-4184 and B-4185). SIPRI reports that one of the Learjet 36As was provided with a side-looking airborne radar (SLAR) already fitted. The five aircraft were delivered in 1987.

PLAAF service

Once in PLAAF service, the Learjets were converted into specialized electronic intelligence (ELINT) aircraft and assigned to the 102nd Air Regiment at Beijing/Nanyuan. Major modifications included the addition of prominent fairings containing surveillance equipment on either side of the mid-fuselage.

Surveillance and reconnaissance roles

Unconfirmed reports suggest that the aircraft were used for surveillance missions along the borders with India and Vietnam and that, in the 1990s, they were used for reconnaissance missions to monitor British military objectives in Hong Kong before the handover of the Special Administrative Region to Beijing.

Recent deployments

The Learjets appear to have been at least partly replaced in their primary ELINT role by specialized versions of the Y-8 High New series. More recently, there are reports that at least one of the aircraft has been used as a transport, although it retains the mid-fuselage reconnaissance pods.

Learjet 35A

A PLAAF Learjet, registration number HY986/B-4186. These aircraft have performed ELINT missions over Vietnam, Taiwan and Hong Kong (prior to the 1997 hand-over).

Learjet 35A

Weight (maximum take-off): 8165kg (18,000lb)
Dimensions: Length 14.83m (48ft 8in), Wingspan 12.04m (39ft 6in), Height 3.73m (12ft 3in)
Powerplant: Two Garrett TFE731-2-2B turbofans, 16kN (3,500lbf) thrust each
Maximum speed: 872km/h (542mph)
Range: 4488km (2789 miles)
Ceiling: 14,000m (45,000ft)
Crew: 2 (pilot and co-pilot); 6 passengers

SPECIAL MISSION AIRCRAFT

Tupolev Tu-154

The PLAAF's 34th Transport Division operates a handful of highly secretive Tu-154Ms, modified versions of the Soviet-era long-haul airliner known to Western intelligence as 'Careless'.

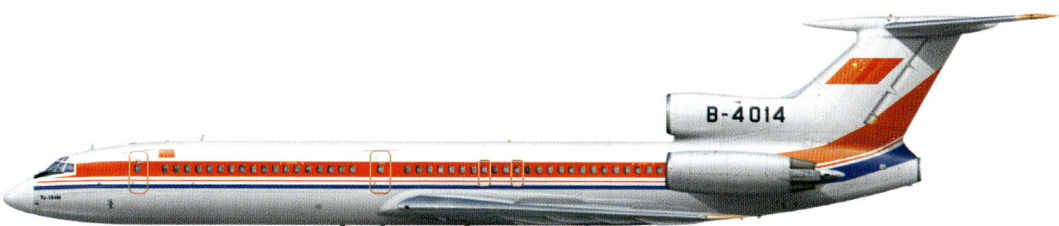

Tupolev Tu-154M/D
A PLAAF Tu-154M, serial number 90A-847, as seen at Nanning Wuxu International Airport, Guangxi Autonomous Region, in October 2017.

In Chinese military service, the dedicated electronic intelligence (ELINT) version of the Tu-154M is known as the Tu-154M/D. The aircraft were acquired by the PLAAF from the civilian China United Airlines.

The initial configuration was the Type I, of which at least four examples were operational from the beginning of 1995.

Type II standard configuration
The aircraft was then modified to Type II standard from around 2013. There are also accounts stating that a further five Tu-154Ms were converted to the same standard, having been withdrawn from VIP transport duties. The Type II aircraft is fitted with a large canoe-shaped fairing under the forward fuselage, believed to contain a synthetic aperture radar (SAR) to provide high-resolution ground-mapping images.

As well as ground reconnaissance, the Tu-154M/D is equipped with a range of long-range ELINT sensors.

These are used to eavesdrop on hostile radio signals, which can be detected, located and then analyzed.

ELINT and accompaniment roles
In particular, the Tu-154M/D Type II aircraft is used for ELINT missions over the East China Sea, close to Japan. When Beijing declared a new Air Defence Identification Zone (ADIZ) over a wide area of the East China Sea in November 2013 and covering the Senkaku Islands, which are also claimed by Japan, Tu-154M/D Type IIs were immediately sent to patrol the area.

Bomber accompaniment
The aircraft is also sometimes used to accompany H-6K bombers over the East China Sea. In this capacity, the H-6Ks are likely used to trigger responses from potentially hostile air defences, which are then monitored by the Tupolev's ELINT sensors, to develop an electronic order of battle.

Tupolev Tu-154M/D
Weight (maximum take-off): 100,000kg (220,462lb)
Dimensions: Length 47.923m (157ft 3in), Wingspan 37.55m (123ft 2in), Height 11.40m (37ft 5in)
Powerplant: Three Aviadvigatel D-30KU-154 II turbofans, each rated 102.96kN (23,149lb) thrust at take-off
Cruising speed: 935km/h (581mph)
Range: 6500km (4039 miles); with maximum fuel load
Ceiling: 12,100m (39,698ft)
Crew: 4 (pilot, co-pilot, navigator and flight engineer)

SPECIAL MISSION AIRCRAFT

Shaanxi KJ-200

Fitted with a characteristic 'balance beam' radar above its fuselage, the KJ-200, which has the Western reporting name 'Moth', is one of a handful of different airborne early warning and control (AEW&C) aircraft types in the PLAAF inventory.

The KJ-200 is alternatively known as the Y-8W and it also has a designation in the Gaoxin, or High New programme series, namely Y-8GX-5. This series includes various special-mission versions of the Y-8 and Y-9 intended for AEW&C, electronic warfare, electronic intelligence, signals intelligence, communications relay and more.

Early development
Development of the KJ-200 began in the late 1990s. It is not clear if it was intended as a less expensive back-up to the more ambitious KJ-2000 'Mainring', which is based on the four-turbofan Il-76 airframe, or if it was always expected to serve as a 'tactical' complement to that more capable aircraft.

It also appears that the KJ-200 was the first of the High New aircraft to be based on the Category III transport

Shaanxi KJ-200A
This KJ-200A, serial number 30672, is designed for airborne warning and control (AWAC) duties, and is part of the 26th Division, PLAAF.

(equivalent to the Y-9 transport) from the outset rather than the previous Y-8 airframe. It is noteworthy that all High New aircraft retain Y-8GX-series designations, regardless of whether they are based on the Y-8 or Y-9 airframe. Initially, however, an older Y-8F200 airframe was used as a testbed for the KJ-200's new radar and was seen under test as of late 2004, although a first flight was reportedly recorded on 8 November 2001.

Equipment configuration
The radar itself is housed in a prominent fairing mounted on top of the fuselage, similar to the Swedish Saab Erieye. This JY-06 active electronically scanned array (AESA) radar is complemented by smaller antennas on the nose and in the tail cone, apparently to provide full 360-degree coverage.

Additionally, there are fairings on the wingtips and on top of the tailfin accommodating electronic support measures (ESM) antennas. A series of antennas arranged above the forward

Shaanxi KJ-200A
Weight (maximum take-off): 61,000kg (134,482lb)
Dimensions: Length 34m (111ft 6in), Wingspan 38m (124ft 8in), Height 11m (36ft 1in)
Powerplant: Four Zhuzhou WoJiang-6 turboprop engines developing 3169kW (4250hp) each
Maximum speed: 660km/h (410mph)
Range: 5500km (3418 miles)
Ceiling: 10,400m (34,121ft)
Crew: 2 plus 5 mission crew
Avionics: Detection range against fighter sized targets: 300-450km (186–280 miles)

SPECIAL MISSION AIRCRAFT

A KJ-200, serial number 30176, sits on the tarmac at an unknown location.

fuselage are thought to be used for VHF and UHF communications, while likely communications intelligence (COMINT) antennas are located below the forward fuselage.

Starting with the second prototype – first flown in January 2005 – the KJ-200 was standardized on the improved Category III airframe, with its solid nose, and also featured a revised tail section, with the rear ramp deleted. The Category III aircraft also has new six-blade propellers, increased internal fuel and a digital flight deck for two flight crew.

The loss of the second prototype in an accident in 2006 appears to have led to delays in the KJ-200 programme. The findings of the accident also appear to have led to some redesign work, including adding vertical endplates on the horizontal tail surfaces for more stability. At the same time, the fuselage was reportedly strengthened. The KJ-200 entered PLAAF service with the 76th Electric Warfare Regiment within the PLAAF's 26th Special Mission Division at Wuxi/Shuofang, serving alongside the larger KJ-2000. Examples are also flown by the People's Liberation Army Navy.

In late 2016, an improved version of the aircraft appeared: the KJ-200A. This version is distinguished by a revised nose containing a new (reportedly weather) radar rather than the previous Pinocchio-type thimble radome. Existing KJ-200s are apparently being modified to KJ-200A standard.

For some time, there was much confusion about the future of the KJ-200 programme. Some accounts suggested it would be abandoned altogether in favour of the KJ-500 AEW&C and its rotodome radar. However, production of both aircraft has continued, and the appearance of a further-improved KJ-200 derivative indicates that the programme is very much still active.

SPECIAL MISSION AIRCRAFT

Shaanxi KJ-200B

The KJ-200B is the latest version of the series, first seen in early 2023. This version features a SATCOM antenna on top of its forward fuselage, a new forward AEW&C antenna in a bigger nosecone similar to that of the KJ-200A, side-looking ESM antennas on its rear fuselage, and a new ESM antenna on top of its vertical tail fin.

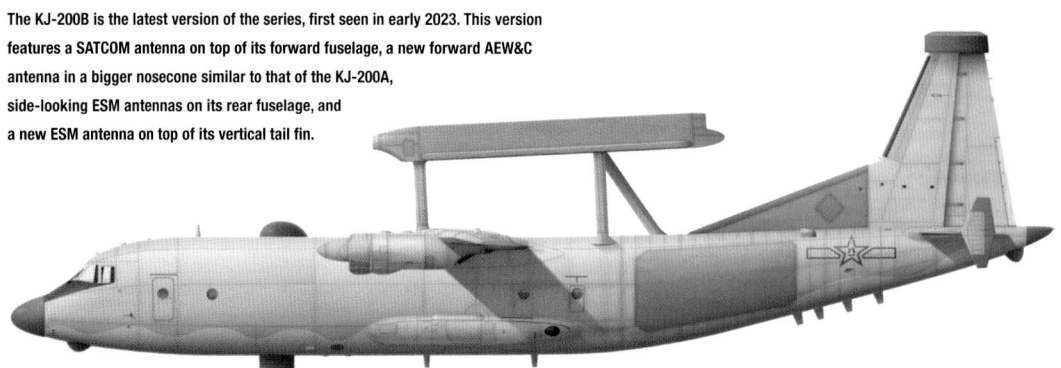

Shaanxi KJ-200H

The KJ-200H is the People's Liberation Army Navy (PLAN) version of the model, with low-visibility finish and insignia.

KJ-200B

The latest KJ-200B appeared in late 2017 and features an apparent satellite communications (SATCOM) 'hump' above the forward fuselage. Below the nose is a turret that reportedly contains an electro-optical/infrared sensor. Below the forward fuselage is another apparent radar, which may well offer ground-mapping and synthetic aperture capabilities. An improved set of ESM antennas is also understood to be included, while the self-protection suite has also reportedly been updated. The KJ-200B was confirmed to be in PLAAF service as of early 2023.

Meanwhile, at least one KJ-200A has also appeared with a fixed inflight refuelling probe mounted above the cockpit. This may be intended for installation on the KJ-200B, or perhaps as a retrofit for both versions of the aircraft. Clearly, the ability to fly longer-range missions would be hugely beneficial for the PLAAF's surveillance missions over the South China Sea and East China Sea.

Another separate High New aircraft has since appeared, with a similar-looking 'balance beam' radar above its fuselage. This is the Y-8GX-12, which may also have the designation Y-9LG. This, however, is an electronic warfare aircraft, with standoff jamming capability, and is discussed separately below.

Shaanxi KJ-200H

Weight (maximum take-off): 61,000kg (134,482lb)
Dimensions: Length 34m (111ft 6in), Wingspan 38m (124ft 8in), Height 11m (36ft 1in)
Powerplant: Four Zhuzhou WoJiang-6 WJ-6 turboprop engines developing 3169kW (4250hp) each
Maximum speed: 660km/h (410mph)
Range: 5500km (3418 miles)
Ceiling: 10,400m (34,121ft)
Crew: 7
Avionics: Detection range against fighter sized targets: 300-450km (186–280 miles)

SPECIAL MISSION AIRCRAFT

Shaanxi KJ-500

Following on from the KJ-200, China developed the KJ-500 as another mid-size airborne early warning and control (AEW&C) aircraft type. The KJ-500 is alternatively known as the Y-9W and has the designation Y-8GX-10 in the Gaoxin or High New programme series.

The vehicle's main characteristic is the primary surveillance radar housed in a more traditional fixed rotodome. While the KJ-500 appeared after the KJ-200 'Moth', it seems that studies for a rotodome-equipped AEW&C predated the 'balance beam' type. As early as the mid-1990s, concepts appeared showing Y-8s fitted with rotodomes, as well as other studies with separate radar arrays in the nose and the tail.

Prototype

After the appearance of concept studies and a wind-tunnel model of a rotodome-equipped Y-8 variant, the first testbed associated with this programme appeared in early 2006. The prototype was not based on the Category III transport (equivalent to the Y-9 transport) but instead used the older Y-8F400 airframe. This retains the previous WJ-6A turboprops driving four-blade propellers, although a Category III-style solid nose replaced the Y-8's original glazed nose. At this stage, the radar was likely a passive electronically scanned array (PESA) type.

The Y-8F400 rotodome testbed appears to have led to the export-oriented ZDK-03, which was procured by Pakistan and is alternatively designated Y-8P Karakorum Eagle. By now, however, the airframe had been switched to the improved Category III platform, including new WJ-6C turboprops driving six-blade propellers.

It seems that the PLAAF's interest was delayed, perhaps as a result of the service already having the KJ-200 fulfilling the same role. Regardless, Beijing placed orders for a domestic version of the rotodome AEW&C type known as the KJ-500.

AESA, radomes and antennas

Compared to the ZDK-03, the KJ-500 has an active electronically scanned array (AESA) radar instead of a PESA type. This is not installed in a rotating rotodome but in a fixed one containing three individual antennas arranged in a triangular configuration, providing 360-degree coverage; the same concept is also used in the larger KJ-2000. On top of the radome is a smaller fairing,

Shaanxi KJ-500

The KJ-500 is another airborne early warning and control (AEW&C) aircraft produced by the Shaanxi Aircraft Corporation. This aircraft, serial number 30077, was spotted at Dafangshen Air Base, China, in August 2022.

Shaanxi KJ-500

Weight (maximum take-off): 70,000kg (154,324lb)
Dimensions: Length 11.50m (37ft 8in), Wingspan 40m (131ft 3in), Height 11m (36ft 1in)
Powerplant: Four Zhuzhou WoJiang-6C (FWJ-6C) turboprop engines developing 3803kW (5100hp) each
Maximum speed: 550km/h (324mph)
Range: 5700km (3542 miles)
Ceiling: 10,500m (34,449ft)
Crew: 5 (flight crew); up to 19 mission crew
Avionics: Detection range against fighter sized targets: 470km (290 mi; 250 nmi)

SPECIAL MISSION AIRCRAFT

apparently concealing a satellite communications (SATCOM) antenna.

Other radomes found elsewhere around the aircraft, such as the most prominent ones on the nose and tail, are likely to provide additional coverage over the forward and rear hemispheres. The aircraft also has an electronic intelligence (ELINT) capability for which it likely relies upon rectangular antennas on each side of the rear fuselage – these fairings are very similar to those found on the Y-9GX-8, a dedicated ELINT platform. For self-protection, the KJ-500 is fitted with countermeasures dispensers below the rear fuselage. In contrast to the KJ-200, the aircraft features a pair of prominent ventral stabilizers below the rear fuselage.

Chinese service

By late 2013, there were at least two KJ-500 prototypes, and the aircraft appears to have entered PLAAF service in late 2014. Around a year later, the People's Liberation Army Navy also introduced the aircraft, designating it the KJ-500H. Production has been carried out at an impressive pace, with reports of as many as 40 aircraft having been completed for both air force and navy use by early 2023.

The aircraft, like the KJ-200, has also begun to sport an inflight refuelling probe. In this form, it is known as the KJ-500A. First identified in early 2018, this is now understood to be the main production version. The KJ-500 has proven to be a popular type with the PLAAF, and its advanced AESA radar likely offers a very similar capability to the much more expensive and complex KJ-2000.

A KJ-500A aircraft arrives at the Zhuhai Air Show Center, Guangdong Province, China, November 2022.

Shaanxi KJ-500A

The KJ-500A is the improved variant with an aerial refueling probe. This aircraft, serial number 30473, was seen at Zhuhai Jinwan Airport, China, in November 2022.

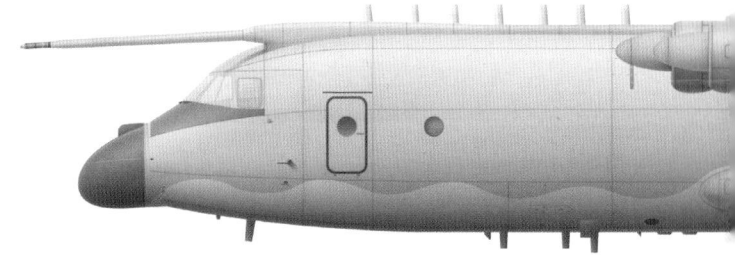

SPECIAL MISSION AIRCRAFT

Shaanxi KJ-500H

The KJ-500H was the version produced for the People's Liberation Army Navy (PLAN). As of 2020, the PLANAF maintained as many as four KJ-500Hs in the Southern Theater at PLA Navy airfields in Lingshui and Yongzhou Lingling.

At the same time, the Y-9 turboprop platform makes the KJ-500 much better suited to deployed operations, including flying to and from smaller airstrips on islands in the South China Sea, for example. Here, its superior short-field performance and ease of maintenance are likely important factors. In 2020, a KJ-500 was seen in satellite imagery on an airstrip in the Spratly Islands, an archipelago in the South China Sea. These disputed islands are also claimed by Malaysia, the Philippines and Vietnam, making the deployment of AEW&C aircraft there highly significant.

KJ-500s are regularly encountered by neighbouring air forces in the Taiwan Strait and South China Sea. In October 2021, for example, China sent what was then a record number of aircraft into this area: 12 H-6 bombers, 34 J-16 fighters, two Su-30s, two KQ-200 anti-submarine warfare aircraft and a pair of KJ-500s. Furthermore, KJ-500s were reportedly also deployed to Tibet during tensions with India along the border with China in 2017.

Shaanxi KJ-500H
Weight (maximum take-off): 70,000kg (154,324lb)
Dimensions: Length 11.50m (37ft 8in), Wingspan 40m (131ft 3in), Height 11m (36ft 1in)
Powerplant: Four Zhuzhou WoJiang-6C (FWJ-6C) turboprop engines developing 3803kW (5100hp) each
Maximum speed: 550km/h (324mph)
Range: 5700km (3542 miles)
Ceiling: 10,500m (34,449ft)
Crew: 5 (flight crew); up to 19 mission crew
Avionics: Detection range against fighter sized targets: 470km (290 mi; 250 nmi)

SPECIAL MISSION AIRCRAFT

Xi'an KJ-2000

Known to Western intelligence as 'Mainring', the KJ-2000 is China's first and – so far – largest dedicated airborne early warning and control (AEW&C) aircraft. Its early production was disrupted by issues surrounding the development of its radar.

The roots of the KJ-2000 lie in China's failed efforts to develop a truly indigenous AEW&C aircraft based on the Shanghai Y-10 four-engine airliner project. After that, Beijing attempted to acquire a Western AEW&C system to be installed on an Il-76 airlifter. The British Argus 2000 was apparently among the radar systems considered, which would have required antennas in separate radomes at the front and rear of the aircraft. After rejecting the British solution, however, China selected a version of the EL/M-2075 Phalcon radar from the Israeli company Elta Electronics. At the same time, Beijing negotiated the purchase of a single A-50 'Mainstay' AEW&C aircraft, minus radar, from Russia – there were also options for three more such aircraft. These were known in Russia as the A-50I (or sometimes A-50AI).

Radar and systems development
In 1999, the first A-50I prototype was delivered to Israel, where it was planned to receive its radar. However, apparently in response to US pressure, Israel withdrew from the deal, leaving the A-50I without a radar and stranded temporarily in Israel. China then had to develop its own radar, known as the Type 88, and the A-50I then arrived in China in 2002 to have it installed. As well as the main radar, carried in a rotodome, the aircraft received a Chinese-made command, control, communications, computers, intelligence, surveillance and reconnaissance (C4ISR) system, including identification friend or foe (IFF) and datalink systems.

New radar
The Type 88 comprises three active electronically scanned array (AESA) antennas arranged in a triangular configuration within a fixed rotodome. It has a reported maximum range of 470km (292 miles). According to reports, the KJ-2000 has a normal flight crew of five as well as carrying up to 11 mission crewmembers.

KJ-2000
The KJ-2000 is an early warning and control system (AEW&C), made up of domestically designed electronics and radars installed on a modified Ilyushin Il-76 airframe. The phased array radar (PAR) carried in a round radome is obvious on this artwork.

SPECIAL MISSION AIRCRAFT

CHINA'S FUTURE AEW&C AMBITIONS

Many rumours indicate that China is now working on a next-generation AEW&C aircraft, which may well be designated KJ-3000, although there is next to no confirmed information about this project. The most that is known is that the new aircraft is likely being developed by Xi'an, and many sources expect it to be built on the basis of the Y-20 airlifter.

In late 2022, a photo appeared showing a model of a version of the Y-20 with large radomes fitted above and below the forward fuselage as well as smaller fairings on the leading edges of the sponsons. However, there is no confirmation that this is actually a model of an AEW&C aircraft since it could also be either a project for an airborne command post, a long-range communications aircraft or some other kind of electronic warfare aircraft altogether.

With that in mind, it remains possible that a future KJ-3000 may carry its main radar antenna (or antennas) in a conventional rotodome housing, much like the KJ-2000. It is also possible that a future AEW&C aircraft for the PLAAF will not be based on the Y-20 at all, with the PLAAF instead waiting for a more economical airliner-type platform to become available.

KJ-2000

Weight (maximum take-off): 175,000kg (385,809lb)
Dimensions: Length 46.6m (152ft 8in), Wingspan 50.5m (165ft 7in), Height 14.8m (48ft 6in)
Powerplant: Four PS-90A turbofan engines developing 157kN (35,300lbf)
Maximum speed: 900km/h (560mph)
Range: 5500km (3418 miles)
Ceiling: 10,200m (6338 miles)
Crew: 5 (flight crew); up to 11 mission crew
Avionics: Detection range against fighter sized targets: 470km (290 mi; 250 nmi); range against ballistic missiles: 1,200km (750 mi; 650 nmi); max simultaneous targets tracked: 60–100

SPECIAL MISSION AIRCRAFT

A KJ-2000 early warning and control system (AEW&C) aircraft performs at the Airshow China 2014 in Zhuhai, Guangdong Province.

While looking broadly similar to the A-50, the KJ-2000 does exhibit certain minor differences, in addition to the non-rotating main radome, which is larger than on the Russian aircraft. The large horizontal strakes found on the A-50's main undercarriage fairings are also removed, being replaced by a pair of canted trapezoidal fins on the rear of the fuselage. The KJ-2000's wingtips also carry two semi-circular antennas, the function of which is unclear. Finally, the satellite communication (SATCOM) fairing on top of the fuselage is of a different, more bulged design than on the Russian aircraft.

Small fleet

The first KJ-2000 prototype took to the air on 11 November 2003. Four more Il-76MD aircraft were transferred to the PLAAF from China United Airlines and were similarly converted as KJ-2000s. The first two examples were delivered to the PLAAF in 2005 and became operational in late 2007. Ultimately, the original A-50I/KJ-2000 prototype had its rotodome removed and became an engine testbed.

This leaves the PLAAF with a fleet of just four KJ-2000s. They serve with the 76th Electric Warfare Regiment within the PLAAF's 26th Special Mission Division at Wuxi/Shuofang. From this base, the aircraft can patrol the strategically vital Taiwan Strait as well as airspace around Japan. It seems almost certain that, had more Il-76 (or A-50) airframes been available, China would have converted more of these as KJ-2000s. However, efforts to acquire additional examples of these aircraft were repeatedly frustrated, and instead, the PLAAF introduced the turboprop-powered KJ-200 and KJ-500 types. There is now, however, growing expectation that a new-generation, jet-powered AEW&C aircraft will follow in due course.

SPECIAL MISSION AIRCRAFT

Shaanxi Y-8 & Y-9 Special Mission Versions

Somewhat confusingly, special mission versions based on both the Y-8 and the new-generation Y-9 transports use designations in the Y-8 Gaoxin, or High New programme series.

For the purposes of this book, however, they are separated into those that use the original Y-8 airframe (Category I and II Platforms) and those that utilize the Y-9/Category III Platform. The following are the primary special mission aircraft based on the original Y-8. Among them are some that are operated exclusively by the People's Liberation Army Navy (PLAN), which are included here for the sake of completeness.

Y-8J 'Mask'

As well as the better-known KJ-200 and KJ-500, there is another airborne early warning version of the Y-8 first noted in 2000, although its command-and-control capabilities are likely far more limited. The Y-8J, known to Western intelligence as 'Mask', is based on the Y-8C transport and is used for maritime surveillance. The original glazed nose is replaced by a large, somewhat drooped radome, the rear cargo ramp is removed and a pressurized cabin is provided for the mission crew. The radar itself is a British-made Racal Skymaster pulse-Doppler type with a reported range of 230km (143 miles) against a sea-surface target and the ability to track 100 aerial targets and 32 sea-surface targets simultaneously. Just four Y-8Js are thought to be in PLAN service.

Y-8GX-1

The Y-8GX-1, also known as the Y-8CB, is an electronic intelligence (ELINT) platform based on the Category I Platform and first identified in 2005. Its primary recognition feature is a long ventral 'canoe' fairing below the forward fuselage, likely housing a large ELINT antenna. Additional smaller antennas are found on the (sealed) rear ramp as well as above and below the fuselage, between the main undercarriage fairings.

The main ELINT array is thought to be able to detect, record, locate, and analyze hostile radio-frequency signals and communications. Some aircraft are also fitted with a dorsal satellite communications (SATCOM) antenna, while the improved Y-8DZ subvariant features additional large rectangular

Shaanxi Y-8JZ Mist

The Y-8JZ is based on the Y-8 'Category III' platform powered by four WJ-6C turboprop engines. As an electronic intelligence gathering (ELINT) aircraft it features four large rectangular bar shaped ESM/ELINT antennas on both sides of the forward and rear fuselage.

89

SPECIAL MISSION AIRCRAFT

Shaanxi Y-8J
The Y-8J is the airborne early warning and control (AEW&C) system variant of the Y-8, developed under Project 515. The type was first sighted near Shanghai in 2000. Uniquely, it features a British Racal Skymaster L-band pulse-doppler search radar, housed in a prominent bulbous and partially drooped nose radome.

Shaanxi Y-8GX-2
This Y-8 GX-2 is the long-range electronic countermeasures (ECM/SOJ) variant of the type. This particular aircraft was seen in October 2020.

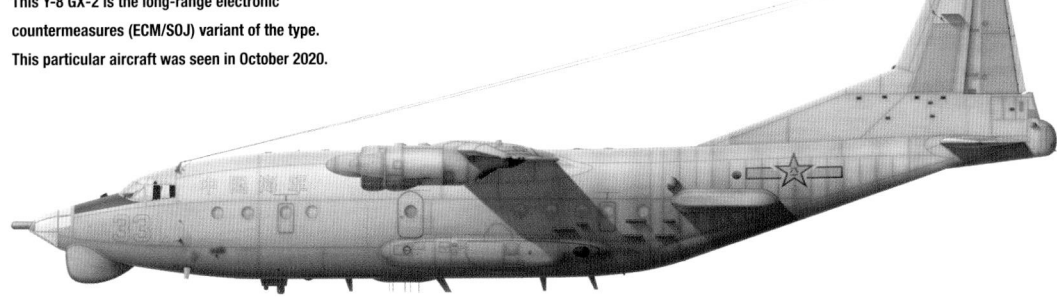

ELINT or electronic support measures (ESM) fairings on the sides of the rear fuselage, plus more antennas on the sides of the forward fuselage and a rear-facing one atop the tailfin. All Y-8GX-1s serve with the PLAAF.

Y-8GX-2
Alternatively known as the Y-8JB and assigned the Western reporting name 'Mace', the Y-8GX-2 is another ELINT platform based on the Category I Platform, although it appears to serve with the PLAN rather than the PLAAF, suggesting it is a dedicated naval version of the Y-8GX-1.

First noted in 2004, it has a large chin-mounted radome likely containing an ELINT antenna or possibly a surface-search radar. There is also a SATCOM antenna in a large dorsal fairing ahead of the tailfin. Additionally, grid-type antennas are fitted on top of the fuselage and at the tip of the

Shaanxi Y-8GX-2 (estimate)
Weight (maximum take-off): 61,000kg (134,100lbs)
Dimensions: Length 34.02m (111ft 7in), Wingspan 38m (124ft 7in), Height 11.16m (36ft 7in)
Powerplant: Four WJ-C turboprops, developing 3170kW (4250hp)
Maximum speed: 660km/h (410mph)
Range: 5615km (3489 miles)
Ceiling: 10,400m (34,120ft)
Crew: 5; 12–18 mission crew
Avionics: BM/KZ800 ELINT array, with antennas in nose and on top of fuselage, plus SATCOM and other communications equipment

SPECIAL MISSION AIRCRAFT

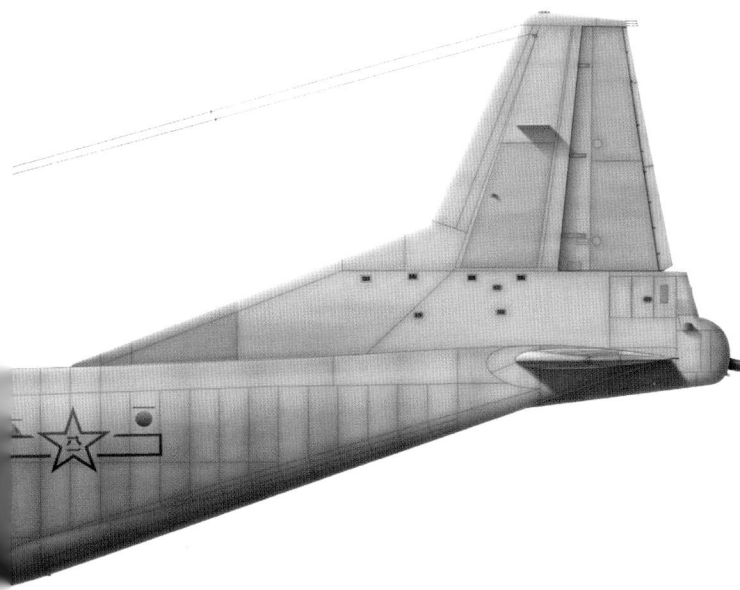

Shaanxi Y-8J (estimate)
Weight (maximum take-off): 61,000kg (134,100lbs)
Dimensions: Length 34.02m (111ft 7in), Wingspan 38m (124ft 7in), Height 11.16m (36ft 7in)
Powerplant: Four WJ-C turboprops, developing 3170kW (4250hp)
Maximum speed: 660km/h (410mph)
Range: 5615km (3489 miles)
Ceiling: 10,400m (34,120ft)
Crew: 5; 12–18 mission crew
Avionics: Racal Skymaster pulse-Doppler radar in under-nose radome with estimated radar range of 230km (143 miles)

nose. Inside the pressurized cabin, the aircraft is understood to have at least four consoles for mission operators.

Like the Y-8GX-1, some of these aircraft appear to have been upgraded with large rectangular ELINT or ESM fairings on the sides of the rear fuselage, plus another rear-facing antenna atop the tailfin. Although unconfirmed, there are reports that development of some of the Y-8GX-2's systems was aided by intelligence exploitation of the US Navy EP-3 Aries II aircraft that force-landed on Hainan Island after a collision with a Chinese J-8 fighter in April 2001.

Y-8GX-3
The Y-8GX-3 is also known as the Y-8G and has the Western reporting name 'Mouse'. It is a long-range electronic countermeasures (ECM) aircraft, this time based on the Y-8 Category II Platform, with a solid rather than a glazed nose and with the normal undernose radome removed. First appearing in 2005, the Y-8GX-3 has two large 'hamster cheek' fairings on the sides of the forward fuselage that likely house ECM antennas to provide long-range standoff electronic jamming capabilities. There is also a large fairing atop the tailfin and a cylindrical fairing below the forward fuselage. These aircraft serve with the PLAAF.

Y-8GX-4
Based on the Y-8 Category I Platform, the Y-8GX-4 or Y-8T is thought to be an airborne command post and was first identified in 2004. The rear fuselage is redesigned, with the tail turret and loading ramp removed.

Multiple communication antenna arrays are located along the top and bottom of the fuselage as well as on the vertical tailfin. A dorsal fairing likely contains a SATCOM antenna. A handful of these aircraft serve with the PLAAF.

Y-8GX-7
Alternatively known as the Y-8XZ, this aircraft is a psychological warfare version equivalent to the US Air Force's EC-130J Commando Solo. First appearing in 2008, it is based on the Y-8 Category II Platform. Key features include large fairings located forward of the main undercarriage bays, as well as prominent plate-like antennas on either side of the rear fuselage. Two blade antennas are fitted on each side of the tailfin, with a wire antenna below the rear fuselage. A large dorsal fairing contains a SATCOM antenna. Used to conduct psychological operations, the Y-8GX-7 has high-power broadcast equipment covering various TV and radio channels over different civilian and military communication bands. As well as broadcasting, the aircraft is also likely able to jam enemy communications. At least two of these aircraft are operated by the PLAAF.

Y-8GX-6
The Y-8GX-6, also known as the Y-8Q – and alternatively as the KQ-200 – is the first of the Y-8/Y-9 special mission versions to be developed for anti-submarine warfare (ASW) duties on behalf of the People's Liberation Army Navy (PLAN).

The aircraft, which apparently has the Western reporting name 'March', was first identified in late 2011. It features a bulbous search radar below

91

SPECIAL MISSION AIRCRAFT

Shaanxi Y-8G
This Y-8G long-range electronic countermeasures (ECM) aircraft, serial number 30518, was seen in October 2020. The type includes SOJ (stand-off-jammer) capabilities, which are designed to confuse and deceive enemy radar signals and communication systems.

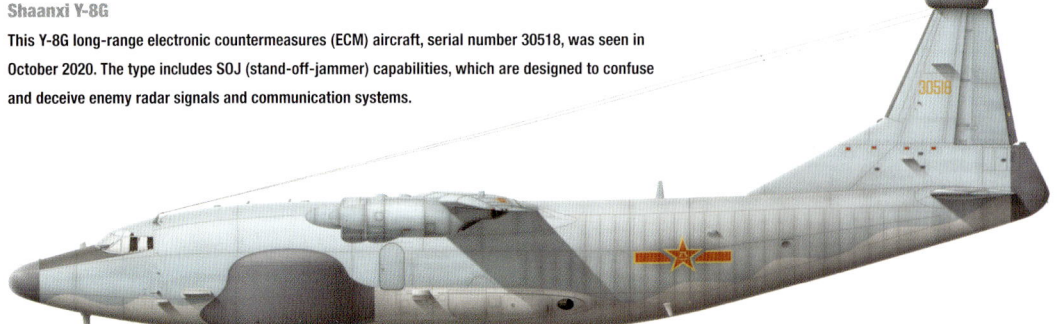

the nose, a lower-fuselage weapons bay ahead of the main undercarriage and a magnetic anomaly detector (MAD) boom on the tail. Other features include an electro-optical turret below the forward fuselage, a radar warning receiver (RWR) and missile approach warning sensors around the airframe, various blade antennas on top of and below the fuselage and two large observation windows in the rear fuselage. The aircraft can deploy sonobuoys to detect underwater contacts, while the weapons bay is thought to accommodate depth charges and torpedoes. The aircraft

A People's Liberation Army Naval Air Force (PLANAF) Shaanxi Y-8GX-4 airborne command post caught on camera in October 2020 while overflying the Taiwan Strait.

reportedly has a range of up to 5000km (3107 miles) and a patrol time of up to 10 hours. Based on the Y-8 Category III Platform, the Y-8GX-6 features a completely pressurized cabin, uprated WJ-6 turboprops driving six-bladed propellers plus small vertical stabilizers on the tailplanes. Deliveries of the 'March' to the PLAN began in 2015.

Y-8GX-8

Alternatively known as the Y-8JZ and seemingly assigned the Western reporting name 'Mist', the Y-8GX-8 was first identified in 2011. It is the first known electronic intelligence (ELINT) aircraft to be based on the Y-8 Category III Platform. Its characteristic features include four large rectangular ELINT or electronic support measures (ESM) antennas located on both sides of the forward and rear fuselage. Further antennas are found in fairings above and below the mid-fuselage, below the nose, on the tail cone, atop the tailfin and on the wingtips. Blade-type antennas are fitted on top of the wing, near the wing root, while an electro-optical turret is located below the fuselage. These aircraft entered service with the PLAN in early 2013, and they are used for regular ELINT missions over the East China Sea near Japan as well as around the Taiwan Strait. The aircraft is today operated by both the PLAAF and PLAN.

Y-8GX-9

The Y-8GX-9 or Y-9XZ was first revealed in late 2012 as a new psychological warfare version based on the Y-8 Category III Platform and expected to replace the Y-8GX-7. Both are broadly equivalent to the US Air Force EC-130J Commando Solo.

While the earlier Y-8GX-7 is understood to be able to broadcast on various TV and radio channels, the Y-8GX-9 is also believed to be able to hack into enemy communication networks, allowing it to interrupt internet traffic and spread false information online. The Y-8GX-9 reportedly entered PLAAF service in 2014. Later aircraft added a satellite communications (SATCOM) antenna above the mid-fuselage.

Y-8GX-11

The Y-8GX-11 or Y-9G is a long-range electronic countermeasures (ECM) aircraft that the US Department of Defense considers to be a likely replacement for the earlier Y-8GX-3 'Mouse'. It was first identified in early 2014. For its standoff jamming role, the Y-8GX-11 has three large oval and rectangular-shaped antennas along each side of the fuselage, as well as two plate-type antennas mounted on the sides of the tailfin. There is also a new chin radome and a cylindrical antenna atop the tailfin. The plate

Shaanxi Y-8XZ (estimate)
Weight (maximum take-off): 61,000kg (134,100lbs)
Dimensions: Length 34.02m (111ft 7in), Wingspan 38m (124ft 7in), Height 11.16m (36ft 7in)
Powerplant: Four WJ-6 turboprops, developing 3170kW (4250hp)
Maximum speed: 660km/h (410mph)
Range: 5615km (3489 miles)
Ceiling: 10,400m (34,120ft)
Crew: 5; up to 12 mission crew

Shaanxi Y-8XZ
This Y-8XZ, serial number 31015, is the psychological operations (PSYOPS) version of the type.

SPECIAL MISSION AIRCRAFT

antennas on the tailfin allow the normal small vertical stabilizers to be removed from the tailplanes. Additionally, an array of blade antennas is found below the fuselage, while small semi-spherical antennas are mounted underneath the wingtips. Reports suggest that the Y-8GX-11 uses solid-state active phased array radar technology to suppress both enemy radar transmissions and communications.

By early 2021, at least six examples were in PLAAF service. These aircraft have been encountered near the Taiwan Strait, in the western Pacific near Japan, as well as having been deployed to the Spratly Islands in the South China Sea.

Y-8GX-12

Alternatively known as the Y-9LG, the Y-8GX-12 is another ECM version based on the Y-8 Category III Platform. It was first identified in satellite imagery in late 2017. Surprisingly considering its assumed role, the Y-8GX-12 has a 'balance beam' radar antenna above its fuselage, as found on the KJ-200 airborne early warning and control (AEW&C) aircraft.

However, it is believed that the radar aboard the Y-8GX-12 is instead used for long-range jamming, using its powerful electronically scanned radar beams to suppress enemy radar

signals. An enlarged nosecone likely contains another electronic warfare (EW) antenna, while side-looking ELINT/ESM antennas seem to be fitted on the sides of the rear fuselage. An apparent SATCOM antenna is located on top of the forward fuselage, while further ESM antennas are mounted underneath the forward and rear fuselage and atop the tailfin. By early 2023, it was reported that the Y-8GX-12 had entered PLAAF service.

Y-8GX-13

The next ELINT variant based on the Y-8 Category III Platform is the Y-8GX-13 or Y-9Z. This aircraft was first identified in late 2017 in satellite imagery.

The aircraft has some similarities to the Y-8GX-11 or Y-9G long-range ECM aircraft, including the two large rectangular-shaped antennas along each side of the fuselage. These are

Shaanxi Y-9YL (estimate)
Weight (maximum take-off): 265,352kg (585,000lb)
Dimensions: Length 36.07m (118ft 4in), Wingspan 38m (124ft 8in), Height 11.3m (37ft 1in)
Powerplant: Four WoJiang WJ-6C turboprop engines each rated at 3805kW (5103hp)
Maximum speed: 650km/h (400mph)
Range: 2200km (1400 miles)
Ceiling: 10,400m (34,100ft)
Crew: 4
Capacity: In medical evacuation configuration, up to 72 stretcher patients plus three medical attendants, or 98 walking wounded

Shaanxi Y-9YL
This Y-9YL, serial number 10256, has been adapted for medical evacuation (medevac) purposes. This aircraft was seen in Zhuhai Jinwan in October 2021.

SPECIAL MISSION AIRCRAFT

Shaanxi Y-9Q
The Y-9Q is the anti-submarine warfare (ASW) variant of the type.

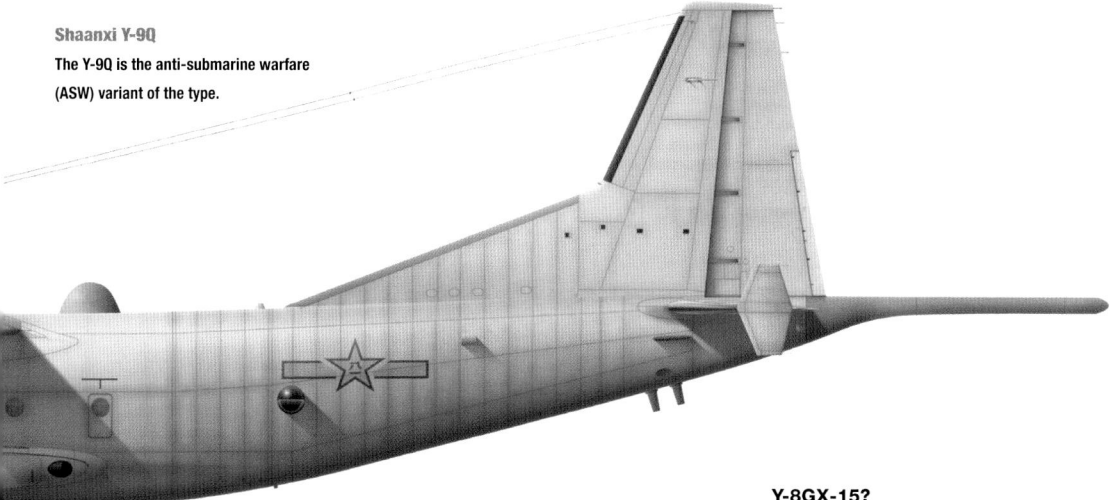

presumed to contain ELINT/ESM arrays. Furthermore, an oval-shaped ESM antenna is mounted on top of the tailfin, with a SATCOM antenna installed on top of the mid-fuselage.

Below the forward fuselage is another antenna array, which may provide synthetic aperture radar (SAR) capabilities. On the sides of the fuselage are 'towel rail' type antennas, which may be used for psychological warfare operations (although this is unconfirmed).

All in all, the complex antenna configuration suggests that the Y-8GX-13 may be intended as a multi-purpose EW aircraft capable of flying missions including gathering ELINT, SAR ground surveillance, communication jamming and psychological warfare. The Y-8GX-13 is thought to have entered PLAAF service by early 2022 and, as of 2023, had begun flying missions in the western Pacific near Japan and Taiwan.

Y-8GX-14

The exact function of the Y-8GX-14 or Y-9T is unclear, but when it was first revealed in mid-2020, observers suggested it was likely intended for communications relay. In particular, it was assumed that the aircraft was intended to fulfil a similar role to the US Navy's E-6B Mercury, providing a long-range communications link with submerged submarines. This ensures a reliable nuclear deterrent can be maintained even if command centres on land are knocked out.

In the PLAN context, the Y-8GX-14 would provide secure and survivable communications with the Type 094 nuclear ballistic missile submarines (SSBNs). Therefore, the Y-8GX-14 is presumed to be equipped with an onboard VLF transmitter and a trailing wire antenna that can be reeled out from the tail cone.

A longer VLF trailing wire antenna is likely installed below the rear fuselage. There are also large conformal ESM antennas on both sides of the rear fuselage and additional antennas on the wingtips. An oval-shaped ESM antenna is fitted atop the tailfin. The Y-8GX-14 is thought to have first taken to the air in 2020, although its current status with the PLAN is less clear.

Y-8GX-15?

The Y-9Q is a new-generation ASW aircraft, presumably intended to supplement and perhaps eventually replace the Y-8GX-6/Y-8Q/KQ-200 aircraft. It is thought to have the Y-8GX-15 designation in the High New series, but this is unconfirmed. The Y-9Q has many similarities with its predecessor, but the nose has been reconfigured, likely now containing a new multi-mode active electronically scanned array (AESA) radar. Two air scoops are located behind the nose to provide cooling air for onboard systems. The MAD 'sting' on the tail is shorter than on the Y-8GX-6, and a SATCOM antenna is fitted above the mid-fuselage.

Additional antennas, likely for ESM arrays, are found on the wingtips. Reports suggest that a rear-facing surface search radar might also be fitted below the MAD. New types of MAWS sensors are located on the forward fuselage, and the aircraft may have the ability to carry anti-ship missiles below the wings as well as depth charges and torpedoes in the weapons bay.

In early 2023, it was reported that the Y-9Q had entered PLAN service.

HELICOPTERS

Chinese helicopters have largely come from foreign sources; the first Chinese production helicopter, the Harbin Z-5, was a licence-built Soviet Mil Mi-4. Following the Sino-Soviet split, China looked elsewhere for its helicopters and the Z-8 and Z-9 were both derived from French designs and in developed form remain in Chinese production today. Although the indigenous Z-20 was 'inspired' to a greater or lesser degree by the Sikorsky UH-60, the Z-10 attack helicopter is an original Chinese design and demonstrates the increasing strength of the Chinese rotorcraft industry.

- Aérospatiale/Eurocopter AS332/EC225 Super Puma
- Mil Mi-17 and Mi-171
- Changhe Z-8
- Harbin Z-9
- Changhe Z-10
- Harbin Z-20

A Z-20 helicopter takes part in a display at the 14th China International Aviation and Aerospace Exhibition in Zhuhai, Guangdong Province, November 2022.

HELICOPTERS

Aérospatiale/Eurocopter AS332/ EC225 Super Puma

A highly successful French medium lift helicopter design, the Super Puma was developed in the mid-1970s and is operated by the PLAAF as a transport and VIP transport.

This aircraft, produced by Aérospatiale a follow on to its successful SA 330 Puma, was powered by a pair of Turbomeca Makila turboshaft engines, replacing the Turbomeca Turmos of the original Puma. The four-bladed main rotor was redesigned to make use of composite materials, and considerable effort was put into improving the new model's crashworthiness and resistance to battle damage.

Maiden flight and usage

Making its first flight in 1978, the Super Puma proved more successful than its forebear, with around 1000 being constructed and further developed versions remaining in production to the present day. It was popular with both military and civil operators, with over thirty nations adopting the type for their armed forces.

China acquired a small fleet of AS332L-1s in 1986, and six are believed to remain in service in 2023. Finished in an attractive white and blue colour scheme, in place of the camouflage colours in which they were originally delivered, the AS332s are mainly used for VIP transport and have been upgraded with modern Chinese equipment, such as an antenna for use with the BeiDou Navigation Satellite System.

In addition, three examples of the larger EC225 (currently in production as the Airbus Helicopters H225) have been acquired and are utilized in the same role. The EC225 features a pair of the more powerful Makila 2A turboshaft engines along with a new five-bladed main rotor, redesigned main gearbox and integrated flight display system.

Eurocopter AS332L Super Puma
This Eurocopter AS332L Super Puma (serial number 2155) serves with the PLAAF.

Eurocopter AS332L Super Puma
Weight (Maximum take-off): 9000kg (19,840lb)
Dimensions: Length 18.70m (61ft 4in), Rotor diameter 15.08m (49ft 6in), Height 4.92m (16ft 1in)
Powerplant: Two 1325kW (1755shp) Turboméca Makila turboshaft engines
Maximum speed: 277km/h (172mph)
Range: 851km (529 miles)
Ceiling: 5180m (16,990ft)
Crew: 2
Capacity: 24 passengers plus attendant or 4490kg (9899lb) payload

Mil Mi-17 and Mi-171

One of the world's most successful helicopters, the Soviet Mi-17 has been produced in vast numbers and remains ubiquitous in the air arms of many nations. China is no exception and has ordered new examples of the Mi-171 – the more modern variant of the Mi-17 – as recently as 2019.

The Mi-17, which first appeared in 1975, is the designation given to export variants of the venerable Mil Mi-8, which first flew in July 1961, the same aircraft being referred to as the Mi-8MT in Soviet/Russian service. Differing from earlier Mi-8 variants in that it is fitted with larger Klimov TV3-117MT engines, rotors, and transmission – along with fuselage improvements for heavier loads – the Mi-17 was adopted by a huge number of nations and is currently in the military inventories of over 70 worldwide.

Most Chinese Mi-17s and Mi-171s have been utilized by the People's Liberation Army Ground Forces Aviation component, though comparatively small numbers also serve with the PLAAF.

Mi-171 upgrades

China acquired its first 24 Mi-17s in 1991 as a replacement for its obsolete Z-5s (a licensed Chinese derivative version of the Mil Mi-4). Originally the intention was to purchase Sikorsky S-70Cs for this purpose, but the US refused to supply these aircraft following the violent response to the Tiananmen square protests of 1989.

The excellent service delivered by this cheap, robust and versatile helicopter saw further batches of Mi-17s purchased followed by 35 of the improved Mi-171 variant in 1995 with a weather radar installed in the chin. Earlier Mi-17s were subsequently upgraded to Mi-171 standard. Several Mi-171s have been upgraded with a search light, IRST turret, flare/chaff launchers and a terrain-following radar in the nose for search and recuse (SAR) missions.

In addition, some Mi-171s had an IR jammer and flare dispenser to protect the helicopter from MANPADS attacks, and a few Mi-171s have been photographed with a SATCOM antenna installed on top of the tail boom. In recent years, Mi-171s have reportedly been providing electronic jamming support for Z-10 attack helicopters utilizing a new ECM pod, first observed in late 2020.

Mil Mi-171

This PLAAF Mi-171, serial number LH99755, was seen at Chelyabinsk Shagol Airport, Russia, in August 2013.

Mil Mi-171
Weight (Maximum take-off): 13,000kg (28,660lb)
Dimensions: Length 25.3m (83ft), Rotor diameter 21.1m (69ft 3in), Height 5.65m (18ft 6in)
Powerplant: Two 1435kW (1924shp) Klimov TV3-117VM turboshaft engines
Maximum speed: 250km/h (155mph)
Range: 610km (980 miles)
Ceiling: 5000m (16,404ft)
Crew: 3
Capacity: 24 troops or 12 stretchers or 4000kg (8818lb) internal payload or 5000kg (11023lb) externally slung

HELICOPTERS

Further variants

A new variant, the Mil-17V5, was introduced to Chinese service in 2001, featuring a solid nose, two improved TV3-117VM engines and a hydraulically operated loading ramp. The two sliding doors on the cabin sides were also enlarged for quicker troop disembarkation. This was followed by the similar Mi-171E in 2006 with improved VK-2500-03 engines, and later examples are fitted with a scissor tail rotor to reduce noise and increase thrust. The most recent version to be ordered is the Mi-171Sh, of which 18 were ordered along with 68 upgraded Mi-171s in 2019. This variant is specifically tailored for the CSAR mission and features an EO turret, armour-protected cockpit and engine compartments, exhaust IR suppressors, 80mm (3.15in) rocket launchers, twin 23mm (0.9in) gun pods and flare/chaff launchers.

Twenty examples of the Mi-17 were also reportedly constructed from Russian components by the Sichuan Lantian Helicopter Company during 2008, with further licensed manufacture expected to follow. Details of these aircraft and the manufacturer are sketchy at best, and there is some doubt whether even the first batch of 20 was completed. Subsequent large orders of helicopters direct from Russia demonstrate that further local production did not continue, if it even occurred in the first place.

Mil Mi-171E

Spotted in April 2022, this Mi-171E includes dark earth, mid green and black/grey tactical camouflage. The yellow code is in the 53x1x range, meaning it belongs to the Western Theatre Command's 5th Transportation and SAR Brigade, based at Chengdu/Qionglai. The helicopter carries both terrain-following radar and an infrared search and track (IRST) system turret.

Mil Mi-171E

Weight (Maximum take-off): 13,000kg (28,660lb)
Dimensions: Length 25.3m (83ft), Rotor diameter 21.1m (69ft 3in), Height 5.65m (18ft 6in)
Powerplant: Two 1790kW (2400shp) Klimov VK-2500-03 turboshaft engines
Maximum speed: 280km/h (170mph)
Range: 800km (500 miles)
Ceiling: 6000m (20,000ft)
Crew: 3
Capacity: 24 troops or 12 stretchers or 4000kg (8818lb) internal payload or 5000kg (11,023lb) externally slung
Armament: Provision for a pintle-mounted machine gun at either or both doors

Mil Mi-171E

This Mi-171E belongs to the Western Theatre Command's Xinjiang Army Aviation Brigade. It is painted in a form of the standard tan/mid green/dark green camouflage, although the tan is noticeably paler than is usual, due to fading.

Changhe Z-8

As a reverse-engineered variant of the amphibious Aérospatiale Super Frelon, the Changhe Z-8's basic design has continued to be developed in China, and updated versions remain in production at the end of 2023 for both civil and military use.

The SA 321 Super Frelon was flown for the first time in 1962 and set an absolute speed record for helicopters at 350.4km/h (217.7mph) the following year. Although only 110 were produced, the type enjoyed long and extensive active service with France, Israel, Libya, Syria, Iraq and South Africa, with the final examples leaving French service as late as 2010. China took delivery of 12 examples between 1975 and 1977 primarily for use in the ASR and SAR roles, designating the helicopter the Z-8. Impressed with the Z-8's performance, the decision was taken to reverse engineer the design and put it into local production.

Role in China

Work on the project began in 1975. Budgetary concerns saw work on Chinese Z-8 production stall for a time, but the first locally produced helicopter flew for the first time in December 1985, with production commencing the following year. As well as its use with Chinese forces, an unspecified number of Z-8s were sold to Sudan. Harbin subsequently developed the Z-8A, a land-based transport, for the People's Liberation Army in the mid-1990s.

This variant utilized more powerful engines, initially dispensed with the stabilizing floats of the original Super Frelon/Z-8 and featured a simplified main undercarriage. Production Z-8As, however, reverted to the original undercarriage, complete with floats, and Z-8As are externally indistinguishable from the earlier model. The Sichuan earthquake of 2008 demonstrated the usefulness of the helicopter for humanitarian missions, and as a direct result, 18 Z-8s were

Changhe Z-8KA
Weight (Maximum take-off): 12,074kg (26,619lb)
Dimensions: Length 19.4m (63ft 8in), Rotor diameter 18.9m (62ft), Height 6.76m (22ft 2in)
Powerplant: Three 1156kW (1550shp) Changzhou WZ-6 (Turbomeca Turmo) turboshaft engines
Maximum speed: 315km/h (196mph)
Range: 820km (510 miles)
Ceiling: 6000m (19,685ft)
Crew: 2–3
Capacity: 27–30 troops or 15 stretchers or up to 5000kg (11,023lb) internal payload

Changhe Z-8KA
This Z-8KA, as seen in November 2008, wears an overall dark olive-green scheme and is coded in the 6x9x range which, at that time, identified it as belonging to the 15th Airborne Army, under direct command of the PLAAF in Beijing. It is Bort White 18 and has the serial number Z8KA-02.

HELICOPTERS

A PLA Z-8 helicopter carries troops somewhere above Hong Kong, August 2020.

ordered by the Chinese People's Armed Police. Most of these have been assigned to forest fire-fighting units and have been used in relief efforts following subsequent earthquakes.

Design improvements

Further development by Harbin saw the proven Z-8 airframe upgraded into a new amphibious utility variant as the Z-8F with Pratt & Whitney Canada PT6A-67B turboshaft engines of greater power than the original Turbomeca Turmo units enabling much improved hot-and-high performance. Other improvements included new composite main rotor blades featuring electric de-icing and new avionics and systems. The Z-8F, as the new variant was designated, flew for the first time in 2004 and is easily distinguishable from earlier versions by its much more streamlined engine intakes and exhausts.

Variants

The late 2000s saw the Z-8 developed into an 18-passenger civil helicopter, the Avicopter AC313, utilizing digital avionics systems and with composites used for around 50 per cent of the airframe. Making its maiden flight in 2010, the AC313 has subsequently been developed into a medium-lift military transport helicopter, confusingly designated both Z-8G and Z-18, which flew in 2014.

The most obvious external change over earlier Z-8 models is that the new helicopter dispenses with the boat-like Super Frelon hull in favour of a largely flat underside with a tail ramp for improved loading.

Known variants of the new helicopter are the basic Z-18 naval transport with folding tail boom and rotor blades and nose-mounted weather radar and FLIR/TV turret, the Z-18A/Z-8G transport with extended nose and nose-mounted terrain-following radar, the Z-8L transport with wide-body fuselage and enlarged fuel sponsons (first reported in January 2019), the Z-18F with chin-mounted surface search radar and dipping sonar and capable of carrying up to four lightweight torpedoes and 32 sonobuoys for the ASW role, and the Z-18J AEW version, which carries retractable radar antennae in place of the rear ramp.

Changhe Z-8K

This Z-8K, with a code in the 51x1x range, identifies it as belonging to the Eastern Theatre Command's Transportation and Search and Rescue Brigade, based at Nanjing. It is Bort Yellow 71 and carries the serial Z8K-01 on the tail rotor pylon. It is finished in a three-tone disruptive scheme with additional red cross markings.

Harbin Z-9

Developed from the French Dauphin 2, over 200 examples of the Z-9 have been built to date, and the type has been widely exported.

Aérospatiale flew its Dauphin 2 for the first time in 1975, and the helicopter proved highly successful – over 1000 were built, and the type remains in production in developed form as the Airbus Helicopters H155. China acquired a licence to produce the Dauphin 2 in July 1980, and Harbin Aircraft Manufacturing Company (HAMC) flew the first locally assembled helicopter the following year, which was designated Z-9.

After constructing an initial batch of 28 helicopters from French components, HAMC produced the largely indigenous multi-role Z-9B with the more powerful Zhuzhou Aeroengine Factory WZ-8A (a licence-produced Turbomeca Arriel) turboshaft engine.

Z-9W and Z-9C

These were followed by the armed Z-9W with optional weapons pylons, gyro stabilization and a roof-mounted optical sight. This aircraft first flew in 1987, with the first weapons tests taking place in 1989. This variant was further developed into the Z-9WA, a night-capable version with nose-mounted FLIR capable of utilizing various anti-tank, anti-ship and air-to-air missiles in concert with a Chinese-developed helmet-mounted sight.

A naval variant, the Z-9C, is a licenced version of the Eurocopter AS565 Panther utilized for SAR and ASW duties. The Pakistan Naval Air Arm also operates the type from its Zulfiquar frigates as the Z-9EC.

Z-19

As well as being produced for various civil roles, the Z-9 has also been developed into the Z-19 light reconnaissance/attack helicopter, with a redesigned forward fuselage incorporating tandem cockpits for pilot and gunner. It is in service with People's Liberation Army Ground Force Aviation units.

Harbin Z-9C

This PLA Navy (PLAN) Z-9 served aboard the Type 054A missile frigate *Zhoushan* (529). It was recorded leaving the flight deck of British frigate HMS *Cornwall* in August 2009, following joint anti-piracy operations in the Gulf of Aden.

Harbin Z-9C

Weight (Maximum take-off): 4100kg (9039lb)
Dimensions: Length 12.11m (39ft 9in), Rotor diameter 11.94m (39ft 2in), Height 4.01m (13ft 2in)
Powerplant: Two 632kW (848shp) Zhuzhou Aero-engine Factory WZ-8A (Turbomeca Arriel) turboshaft engines
Maximum speed: 305km/h (190mph)
Range: 1000km (620 miles) with auxiliary fuel tank
Ceiling: 4500m (14,800ft)
Crew: 1–2
Capacity: 10 passengers or up to 1900kg (4189lb) payload

HELICOPTERS

Changhe Z-10

Initially developed by Harbin in concert with the Kamov Design Bureau during the 1990s, the Z-10 would become China's standard medium attack and anti-tank helicopter, with over 200 aircraft in service.

The Z-10 utilized significant input from foreign companies, including Eurocopter and Agusta Westland as well as Pratt & Whitney, who was later found guilty of unlawfully providing US military technology to the Z-10 programme. Pressure of work at Harbin saw the project passed to Changhe in 2000, and the Z-10 was flown for the first time in April 2003.

Technical features

The Z-10 adopts the conventional stepped tandem cockpit design of most helicopter gunships and features a 23mm (0.9in) PX-10A chain gun mounted under the chin. This is aimed by the gunner in the forward cockpit by helmet-mounted display. The aircraft's main weapons are eight KD-9 or KD-10 laser-guided anti-tank missiles carried on the weapons pylons slightly aft of the pilot's cockpit and, comparable to the American AGM-114 Hellfire, possessing a secondary anti-helicopter capability. Along with the TY-90 missile, which is specifically designed for use

Changhe Z-10K
This Z-10K belongs to the 4th (Rotary Wing) Brigade of the PLAAF, based at Huangpi. It wears a three colour tactical camouflage and carries AKD-10 anti-tank missiles under its stub wings. These are carried in sets of four hung from each pylon, but only the nearest two of the outboard set are visible in the artwork.

by helicopters in aerial combat, the BA-21 long-range anti-tank missile may also be carried, which can be fired from up to 17.7km (11 miles) away.

Production

Production Z-10s entered service in 2012. Since then, the helicopter has been subject to an upgrade programme that saw upward-pointing engine exhaust nozzles added to reduce the helicopter's infrared signature, and additional armour plates added to the cockpit and engines. A new IFF system and antenna for the BeiDou satellite navigation system were also added.

An upgraded export version designated the Z-10ME was unveiled

Changhe Z-10K
Weight (Maximum take-off): 7000kg (15,432lb)
Dimensions: Length 14.15m (46ft 5in), Rotor diameter 12m (39ft 4in), Height 3.85m (12ft 8in)
Powerplant: Two 930–957kW (1247–1283shp) AVIC WZ-9 turboshaft engines
Maximum speed: 270km/h (170mph)
Range: 800km (500 miles)
Ceiling: 6400m (21,000ft)
Crew: 2
Armament: One 23mm (0.906in) revolver gun or 25mm (0.984in) chain gun, flexibly mounted under nose; four hardpoints with a total capacity of 1500kg (3307lb), able to carry a variety of gun pods, air-to-ground, and air-to-air guided missiles

in 2018, and in July 2023, an initial order was placed by Pakistan for this aircraft following the US embargo imposed on Pakistan's preferred choice of the Turkish-built T129 ATAK (which uses American engines). Pakistan had previously trialled three Z-10s in 2015 but rejected the design due to the inadequate power of the WZ-9 engine.

HELICOPTERS

Harbin Z-20

Derived from the UH-60, the Harbin Z-20 is comparable to the latest Blackhawk variants in capability and is intended to replace the Mil Mi-17 in PLAAF service.

After acquiring 24 Sikorsky UH-60 Blackhawk helicopters in the 1980s, the US embargoed further deliveries for political reasons in 1989. As a result, an indigenous '10-tonne helicopter project' was initiated, and the resulting aircraft bore an obvious resemblance to Sikorsky's Blackhawk.

Derided as the 'Copyhawk' by some Western commentators, development of the Z-20 was delayed by the greater priority afforded to the Z-10 helicopter gunship and flew for the first time only in December 2013.

Traits and service history
Although externally very similar to the UH-60, the Z-20 differs in certain key regards, most obviously in its use of a five-blade main rotor as opposed to the Blackhawk's four blade unit as well as its fly-by-wire controls.

The main cabin of the Z-20 is believed to be more capacious than that of the UH-60, and from the outset, the helicopter was intended to possess good high-altitude performance, allowing it to operate in mountainous areas.

Variants
Introduced to service in 2019 and in production ever since, an unknown number of Z-20s has been delivered to the PLAAF, and the aircraft is also in service with the Chinese Army and Navy as well as with the civil Chinese People's Armed Police Force.

Variants include the Z-20K SAR/transport helicopter, Z-20F and J, Naval ASW variants, and the Z-20W armed model with provision to carry the AKD-9 and AKD-10 laser-guided air-to-ground missiles. A stealthy Z-20 variant has been reportedly under development since 2015, allegedly derived from analysis in Pakistan of the wreckage of the stealth-oriented Blackhawk that crashed during the assassination of Osama Bin Laden in 2011.

Harbin Z-20
This PLAAF Z-20, registration LH982281, was seen at Zhuhai Jinwan Airport in November 2022.

Harbin Z-20
Weight (Maximum take-off): Approximately 10,000kg (22,000lb)
Dimensions: Length 19.54m (64ft 1in), Rotor diameter 16.2m (53ft 2in), Height 4.98m (16ft 4in)
Powerplant: Two 2000kW (2,682shp) WZ-10 turboshaft engines
Maximum speed: 320km/h (199mph)
Range: 560km (350 miles)
Ceiling: 5400m (17,717ft)
Crew: 2
Capacity: Up to 1000kg (2200lb) of cargo internally, including 12–15 troops, or up to 4000kg (8,800lb) externally slung; may be armed with up to eight KD-10 anti-tank IR guided missiles

---

105

UNMANNED AERIAL VEHICLES

Unmanned Aerial Vehicles (UAVs) have revolutionised tactical and strategic observation and reconnaissance and Chinese companies are global leaders in the civilian drone industry. China is the world's second largest drone market, only the United States is larger. China has produced an impressive array of military drones for a variety of applications. This chapter concentrates on those currently employed by the PLAAF.

- J-6W
- BZK-007 Sunshine
- BZK-005 Giant Eagle
- CH-5 Rainbow
- GJ-1/WD-1K Wing Loong
- GJ-2 Wing Loong II
- WZ-10 Wing Loong 10 (Wind Shadow)
- WZ-10 Cloud Shadow
- WZ-7 Soaring Dragon
- TB-001 Twin-Tailed Scorpion
- WZ-9 Divine Eagle

A technician tests the operation and control system for the Wing Loong 1 unmanned aerial vehicle (UAV) at the assembly plant of Chengdu Aircraft Industry Group (CAIG).

UNMANNED AERIAL VEHICLES

Of the UAVs described in this chapter, none derive from an earlier airframe than the Shenyang J-6W. Essentially a remotely controlled Shenyang J-6 fighter, the manned variant was a Chinese-produced version of the venerable MiG-19, the world's first mass-produced supersonic fighter.

J-6W

The J-6W UAV variant was developed in the late 1990s and entered service during the early 2000s with autopilot, GPS/INS and additional communication equipment installed into a standard retired J-6 fighter. As a result, the J-6W offered a simple and low-cost route to obtain an unmanned combat aerial vehicle (UCAV). It usually carries two 250kg (551lb) general purpose or cluster bombs under its wings for ground attack missions, which can be one-way or a round trip, depending on the expected strength of enemy air defences. The J-6W may also operate as a radar decoy to overwhelm enemy surface-to-air missile systems. The J-6W is very much an outlier in that it utilizes a pre-existing airframe, though the BZK-007 Sunshine admittedly looks like it also does.

BZK-007 Sunshine

Resembling a small private aircraft, the BZK-007 is a low-wing monoplane powered by a piston engine with a 3-blade propeller and able to take off/land autonomously using either a retractable or non-retractable undercarriage. A medium-altitude and long endurance (MALE) UAV, the BZK-007 was codeveloped by the Guizhou Aircraft Industry Corporation (GAIC) and Beijing University of Aeronautics and Astronautics (BUAA) during the early 2000s. A satellite communication (SATCOM) antenna inside a large dorsal bulge provides real-time transmission of data and receives commands from the ground control station. The bulge resembles the cockpit canopy of a conventional aircraft, and though it is not transparent, it is finished in a different shade to the rest of the airframe and further contributes to the BZK-007's visual similarity to a

---

Harbin BZK-005
Weight: 1250kg (2756lb)
Dimensions: Length: 9m (29ft 6in); Wingspan: 19m (62ft 4in)
Powerplant: Conventional gas-fueled engine driving multi-bladed propeller unit at the rear of the fuselage
Range/Endurance: 40 hours
Service ceiling: 8000m (26,000ft)
Speed: 50–180km/h (93–112mph, 81–97kn)
Weapons: Typically none for ISR role; BZK-005C incorporates an ordnance-carrying capability for drop bombs and laser-guided bombs

---

BZK-005 Giant Eagle

A BZK-005 is paraded on the back of a truck during a military parade in Tiananmen Square, Beijing, 3 September 2015.

UNMANNED AERIAL VEHICLES

conventional manned aircraft. The Sunshine is known to have flown reconnaissance missions over the contested South China Sea as well as operating over the Taiwan Strait from September 2022.

BZK-005 Giant Eagle

A contemporary of the BZK-007, though with an external appearance more obviously belying its unmanned configuration, is the BZK-005 Giant Eagle, which was revealed in public for the first time during a video presentation at the 2006 Zhuhai International Airshow. This UAV is intended for medium/high-altitude long-range strategic reconnaissance missions and is capable of a 40-hour endurance. With a twin-boom design and a pusher propeller powered by a piston engine, the aircraft was built in a shape optimized for stealth. The BZK-005 is a large UAV with a 19m (62ft 4in) wingspan and a maximum take-off weight of around 1250kg (2756lb). A SATCOM antenna is thought to be installed inside the prominent 'head' bulge, allowing live data transmission over thousands of kilometres, and a small turret under the nose houses FLIR and CCD cameras. Satellite images have shown that BZK-005s were deployed on the Spratly Islands, a disputed archipelago in the South China Sea, as well as in Tibet for operations along the border with India. It is also known to have flown reconnaissance missions over the East China Sea close to the coastline of Japan and Taiwan.

An improved variant believed to be the BZK-005B has been observed and features a chin-mounted synthetic aperture (SAR) antenna necessitating the relocation of the camera turret to a mid-fuselage position. An armed version has also been developed

CH-5 Rainbow

A CH-5 medium altitude long endurance UAV system on display at the China International Aviation & Aerospace Exhibition, in Zhuhai, China, 2016. It carries AR-1 or AR-2 compact supersonic anti-tank missiles.

Ch-5 Rainbow

Weight: 2,225kg (4,905lb)
Dimensions: Length: 11.2m (36ft 8in); Wingspan: 21m (68ft 10in)
Powerplant: Turboprop
Range/Endurance: 10,600km (6214mi)
Service ceiling: 9,000m (29,500ft)
Speed: 220km/h (137mph)
Weapons: Anti-tank missiles; smart weapons

UNMANNED AERIAL VEHICLES

Wing Loong 1E
A Chengdu GJ-1 unmanned aerial vehicle (UAV), also known as Wing Loong 1E, performs during Airshow China 2022 at Zhuhai Air Show Center.

Chengdu GJ-1
Weight: 1100kg (2425lb)
Dimensions: Length: 9.05m (29ft 8in); Wingspan: 14m (45ft 11in)
Powerplant: One Rotax 914 turbocharged, 75kW (100shp)
Range/Endurance: 4000km (2,485 mi, 2,200 nmi)
Service ceiling: 5000m (16,400ft)
Speed: 280km/h (174mph, 150kn)
Weapons: 200kg (440lb) of air-to-surface weapon

that was first revealed in 2018. Designated the BZK-005C, it features an improved structure and electronic system with both an attack and reconnaissance capability. It can carry bombs or missiles up to a maximum of 300kg (660lb).

A series of Rainbows
Another UCAV intended for the medium-altitude long endurance (MALE) role is the China Aerospace Science and Technology Corporation (CASC) CH-5 Rainbow, one of a series of UAVs and UCAVs named 'Rainbow' that began with 2000's twin-boom CH-1, which directly led to China establishing a UAV programme. Most of the Rainbow series were developed primarily for export with the CH-2, another twin-boom design, and the canard CH-3 following the initial CH-1. The CH-4, however, is virtually identical externally to the General Atomics MQ-9 Reaper and has been further developed into the CH-5, the most recent of the Rainbow series to be produced. It is touted as offering the same capability as the MQ-9 at roughly half the cost, though this claim may be difficult to justify as the piston engine of the CH-5 produces around half the power of the Reaper's turboprop and the aircraft can carry just two AR-1 lightweight air to surface missiles for ground attack and an SAR pod for reconnaissance.

Nonetheless, the CH-4 and 5 have perhaps unsurprisingly proved popular on the export market with Myanmar, Pakistan, Egypt, Saudi Arabia, Algeria and Iraq – nations all known to operate the type. First flying in 2015, the CH-5 is capable of carrying a 1000kg payload and possesses an impressive maximum endurance of 60 hours. Although a small number of CH-4s are in service with the PLAAF, the main user is the People's Liberation Army. The PLAAF has also reportedly taken delivery of a handful of CH-5s.

Wing Loong I
A very similar UCAV, again intended for the MALE role, is the GJ-1/WD-1K Wing Loong (Pterosaur) I developed

by the Chengdu Aircraft Research & Design Institute (CADI) in concert with Chengdu Aircraft Corporation (CAC) and Guizhou Aircraft Industry Corporation (GAIC). Broadly similar in size, layout, mission and capability to the US MQ-1 Predator, the GJ-1 first flew in October 2007.

As well as operating with Chinese forces, it had been exported to 11 other nations by 2023 and has seen active service in several theatres. Powered by a 74.6kW (100hp) ROTAX 914 piston engine, the aircraft features a prominent dorsal bulge at its nose that houses a SATCOM antenna, which allows the UCAV to communicate with a ground control station via satellite, a communication relay UAV or direct signal transmission.

Wing Loong I is fitted with an electro-optical (EO) turret under the nose containing FLIR, TV and laser rangefinder/designator for tracking and locking onto ground targets in all weather conditions. The UCAV can not only supply guidance to its own missiles but also the Precision Guided Munitions (PGMs) launched by other aircraft or ground forces. Wing Loong usually carries a pair of KD-10/BA-7 laser-guided anti-tank guided missiles (ATGMs) as its primary armament, but it can also be fitted with two YZ-100 series 100kg (220lb) cluster bombs instead. Capable of a maximum speed of 280km/h (174mph), Wing Loong possesses a range of 4000km (2485 miles), an endurance of 20 hours and can attain a ceiling of 5000m (16,400ft).

Known to have been in PLAAF service since at least 2014, Wing Loong was the first Chinese UCAV to become operational, though the UAE had reportedly become the type's first export customer in 2012. Saudi Arabia followed suit in 2014, and several Saudi examples have been shot down over Yemen. Pakistan, Kazakhstan, Indonesia, Uzbekistan, Ethiopia and Egypt have all taken delivery of Wing Loongs, with the latter nation reportedly placing an order for

---

Chengdu GJ-2
Weight: 4200kg (9259lb)
Dimensions: Length: 11m (36ft 1in); Wingspan: 20.5m (67ft 3in)
Powerplant: One turboprop engine
Range/Endurance: 32 hours
Service ceiling: 9900m (32,000ft)
Speed: 370km/h (230mph)
Weapons: 480kg (1060lb) of air-to-surface weapon

Wing Loong II

A Chengdu GJ-2 unmanned aerial vehicle (UAV), also known as Wing Loong 2, performs during Airshow China 2022 at the Zhuhai Air Show Center, Guangdong Province, China.

UNMANNED AERIAL VEHICLES

32 improved Wing Loong 1Ds with an Egyptian-built C145 engine of greater power, synthetic aperture radar (SAR) and four weapons pylons capable of carrying double the payload of the original UCAV and possessing an endurance of some 35 hours.

Wing Loong II

Meanwhile, a larger and more powerful UCAV designated the GJ-2 Wing Loong II was being developed by CADI and GAIC. Powered by a turboprop engine, it can carry 12 ATGMs or a payload of up to 400kg (880lb). In addition to the EO turret, Wing Loong II also features an SAR radar in its nose for acquiring ground targets in poor weather, and a datalink antenna for guiding missiles is installed under the starboard forward fuselage. The UCAV is capable of locating, tracking and, if necessary, destroying ground targets, as well as taking off and landing autonomously. Maximum speed is raised to 370km/h (230mph), and Wing Loong II boasts the same 20-hour endurance as its immediate forebear. In December 2017, GJ-2 undertook weapon integration tests, launching various GPS-, laser- and IR-guided missiles and bombs, and more recently, China has reportedly developed ELINT and ASW variants of the design. It is believed that the UAE acquired the first 15 Wing Loong IIs. These have subsequently been involved in the Libyan civil war armed with BA-7 ATGMs and have suffered several losses.

Satellite images have demonstrated that GJ-2s have been in PLAAF service since at least November 2018, based both in Tibet and Xinjiang Province facing India. Nigeria and Ethiopia ordered GJ-2s in 2020 and 2021 respectively, with Algeria, Morocco and Pakistan all reportedly acquiring examples during 2023.

Wind Shadow/Cloud Shadow

A larger, jet-powered UAV has also joined the Wing Loong line-up in the form of the WZ-10 Wing Loong 10.

WZ-10 Cloud Shadow
Weight: 2,300kg (5071lb)
Dimensions: Length: 9m (29ft 6in); Wingspan: 20m (65ft 7in)
Powerplant: Turbojet
Range/Endurance: 90km (180mi)
Service ceiling: 15,000m (49,000ft)
Speed: 620km/h (385mph)
Weapons: Missiles; guided bombs

WZ-10 Cloud Shadow
A Cloud Shadow unmanned aerial vehicle (UAV) is displayed at the China International Aviation & Aerospace Exhibition in Zhuhai, China, 2016.

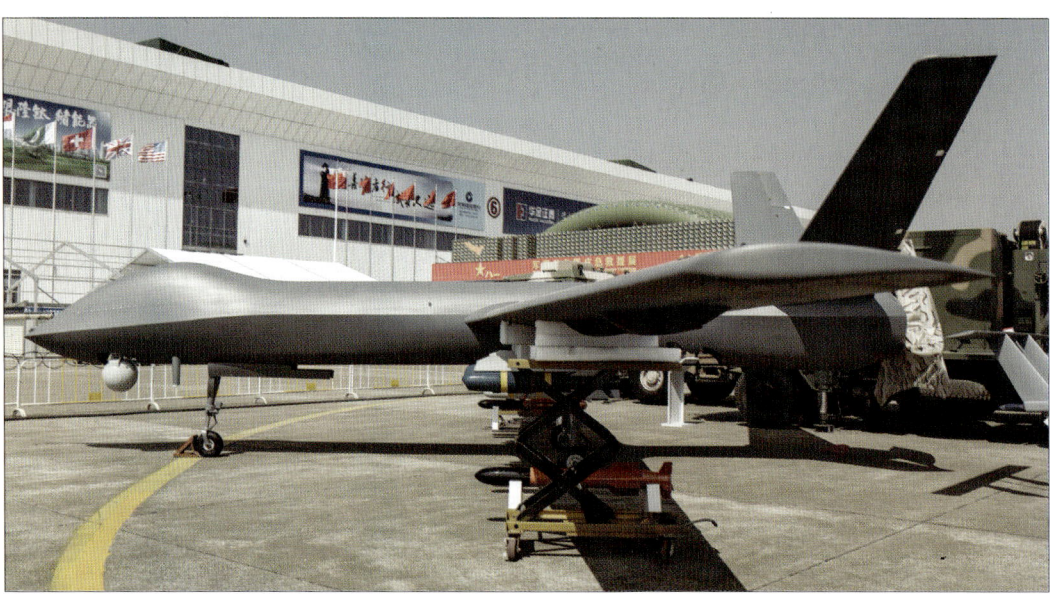

Developed in the late 2000s and early 2010s by CAC and originally named the Sky Wing III, it was described as a high-speed, high-altitude, tactical unmanned aerial vehicle of composite construction that bore a distinct resemblance to the General Atomics MQ-10 Avenger jet-powered UCAV, which was in development in the US at much the same time. Redesigned with improved stealth characteristics, a twin-engine powerplant and increased endurance, the Sky Wing III was renamed the Wind Shadow. This aircraft made its first flight in 2014 and is believed to have entered PLAAF service in 2018. A simpler export-orientated derivative with a single engine was also developed and was named Cloud Shadow, both aircraft being externally indistinguishable from most angles.

Officially designated the WZ-10 in PLAAF service, the name Wing Loong 10 has been applied to the aircraft. A SATCOM antenna is installed within the very pronounced head bulge, and an EO turret can be installed underneath the forward fuselage for the reconnaissance mission. Operational WZ-10s were observed in satellite imagery stationed in Jilin Province, facing North Korea, in June 2023.

Soaring Dragon

All the Wing Loong models are of relatively conventional configuration, but another UAV developed by the partnership of CADI and GAIC, the stealthy WZ-7 Soaring Dragon, intended primarily for the reconnaissance role, features a strikingly unusual airframe design: a box/diamond wing, which is intended to reduce drag and airframe weight whilst increasing lift. Following the construction at CAC of a technology demonstrator in 2011, Soaring Dragon underwent a major redesign, and the resulting WZ-7 features several substantial changes, being smaller in both length and span and featuring twin vertical slanted tails and two ventral fins. A typical 'head' bulge contains SATCOM equipment with the camera compartment immediately behind it.

The engine of the WZ-7 is not definitively known but is speculated to be the Guizhou WP-13 turbojet (a

WZ-7 Soaring Dragon
A WZ-7 high-altitude reconnaissance drone is displayed during Airshow China 2021 in Zhuhai, Guangdong Province, China.

WZ-7 Soaring Dragon
Weight: 2,000kg (4,409lb)
Dimensions: Length: 14.33m (47ft); Wingspan: 24.86m (81ft 4in)
Powerplant: Guizhou WP-13 turbojet
Range/Endurance: 2,000km (1,200mi)
Service ceiling: 18,000m (59,000ft)
Speed: 1000km/h (621mph)
Weapons: Laser-guided bombs; air-to-surface missiles

UNMANNED AERIAL VEHICLES

TB-001
A TB-001, nicknamed "Twin-Tailed Scorpion", unmanned combat aerial vehicle (UCAV) undergoes flight tests.

TB-001
Weight: 2000kg (4409lb)
Dimensions: Length: 10m (32ft 10in); Wingspan: 20m (65ft 7in)
Powerplant: Two turboprops
Range/Endurance: 6000km (3,700mi) / 35 hours
Service ceiling: 9500m (31,170ft)
Speed: 250km/h (155mph)
Weapons: Air-to-surface missiles; laser-guided bombs

Chinese-built Tumansky R-13) –an unusual choice for such an aircraft, as turbojets typically demand a relatively high fuel consumption. The WZ-7 is rumoured to have made its first flight in late 2012, and it reportedly entered production in late 2015, beginning PLAAF service during 2018. In 2019, WZ-7s were deployed in Jilin Province, facing North Korea, and at least five WZ-7s were observed in Tibet in 2020. During 2022, the Soaring Dragon had begun to fly reconnaissance missions over the Taiwan Strait as well as over the Philippine Sea. Around 20 examples of this distinctive UAV have been constructed to date.

Sichuan Tengden Technology
Another company engaged in the production of drones is Sichuan Tengden Technology, previously known as Tengoen Technology, which despite only being founded as recently as 2016 produces several types of UAV all bearing names of characters from the classic Chinese novel 'Water Margin', such as the TB-001 Twin Tailed Scorpion. This drone is currently in service and caused a considerable stir in April 2023 by flying an unprecedented 'island encirclement' flight around Taiwan.

The first product of Sichuan Tengden Technology to be produced, the TB-001 is a fairly large twin-engine aircraft of twin-boom configuration powered by two turbocharged piston engines. Although the Taiwan flight was characterized as a reconnaissance mission, the TB-001 was designed from the outset as an armed UAV and can carry the FT-7 glide bomb, FT-8D guided missile and the FT-9 and FT-10 guided bombs. The TB-001 can reportedly also be equipped with the

18kg (40lb) AR-2 and 73kg (160lb) AR-4 air-to-surface-missile, as well as the 91kg (200lb) AR-3 cruise missile, the C-701/K anti-ship missile or the CM-502 air-to-surface missile.

Capable of staying airborne for 35 hours and flying over 6000km (3700 miles), the TB-001 spans 20m (65ft 7in) and is 10m (32ft 10in) long, a similar size to a typical twin-engine utility aircraft, such as the Beech King Air. The capability of the Twin Tailed Scorpion has been enhanced with the introduction of the TB-001A, which adds a third engine driving a pusher propellor between the tail booms. The added power enables the maximum payload to be increased from 1200kg to 1500kg (3300lb), and that of the service ceiling to be raised from 8000m ((26,250) to 9500m (31,170ft).

Divine Eagle

Larger still is the remarkable WZ-9 Divine Eagle, which is believed to have entered service in the summer of 2023. This is a truly enormous high-altitude long endurance (HALE) drone with a wingspan of approximately 35m (115ft) and a highly unusual layout, with twin fuselages and a wing mounted at the rear. SATCOM antenna is fitted in the port fuselage head bulge, and a single turbofan engine is pylon-mounted on the wing between the fuselages, while a single horizontal control surface joins the two fuselage noses. Developed by Shenyang Aircraft Corporation (SAC), Divine Eagle is intended as an 'anti-stealth' AEW platform. Believed to be fitted with a side-looking conformal radar antenna array in each fuselage, the ultra-wide dual-band electronically scanned radar is intended to be capable of detecting stealth aircraft at long range but is predicted to suffer from low accuracy. A group of WZ-9s would be able to pick up radar reflections from the same stealth aircraft and accurately plot its position through comparatively simple triangulation, effectively acting as an airborne multi-static radar system.

Little is known about Divine Eagle's capabilities, but if successful, the WZ-9 is (so far as is yet known) the world's first airborne anti-stealth radar system and could pose a serious problem for such stealthy aircraft as the F-22, F-35 and B-2.

WZ-9 Divine Eagle
Weight: 15,000kg (33,069lb)
Dimensions: Length: 15.25m (50ft); Wingspan: 40.23m (132ft)
Powerplant: One WP-13 turbojet engine developing 4490kg (9900lb) of thrust, or one Minshan turbojet engine developing 3175kg (7000lb) of thrust
Range/Endurance: Unknown
Service ceiling: Unknown
Speed: Unknown
Weapons: Two hardpoints for guided missiles or precision-guided bombs

---

WZ-9 Divine Eagle

Built by the Shenyang Aircraft Corporation's 601 Institute, China's enormous Divine Eagle UAV is larger than the US Air Force's Global Hawk.

TRAINERS

Current Chinese training aircraft appear to cover a remarkable amount of aviation history with the venerable Nanchang CJ-6, which would not have looked out of place during World War II, still operating as the PLAAF's standard primary trainer – but at the other end of the scale, the fly-by-wire Hongdu JL-10, with its glass cockpit and potent attack capability, is one of the world's most modern trainers. With the exception of the JL-8, which was built with Pakistani co-operation, all operational PLAAF trainers possess considerable Soviet or Russian design influence.

- Nanchang CJ-6
- Hongdu JL-8
- Guizhou JL-9
- Hongdu JL-10

A PLAAF Hongdu JL-10, a supersonic advanced jet trainer, performs during the Zhuhai Airshow in Zhuhai, Guangdong Province, November 2022.

TRAINERS

Nanchang CJ-6

In service since 1960, the Nanchang CJ-6 remains the PLAAF's standard basic trainer over sixty years later. In 2023, at least 400 examples were on strength.

First flown in 1958, the CJ-6 is a Chinese development of the Yak-18 featuring a tricycle undercarriage and new wings. The aircraft is regularly confused with the Soviet Yak-18A, which also features a tricycle undercarriage, though the CJ-6 can easily be distinguished by its angular tail and rudder and pronounced dihedral on the outer wing panels.

Production and roles

More than 3000 CJ-6s are believed to have been built, most of them the improved CJ-6A model that substituted a 212.5kW (285hp) Zhuzhou Huosai radial engine in place of the 194kW (260hp) unit originally fitted, and the aircraft was exported to several friendly nations such as Albania, Bangladesh, Cambodia, North Korea, Tanzania and Sri Lanka. A few examples of a two-seat armed border patrol aircraft were also produced powered by a 223.7kW (300hp) Zhuzhou Huosai HS-6D radial, and the aircraft was also developed for civil applications in the mid-1980s as the 'Haiyan' (Petrel).

Following the prototype Haiyan A, the Haiyan B was intended for agricultural topdressing, aerial spraying, and firefighting, and was followed by the Haiyan C general aviation version. Production of the CJ-6 finally ceased in 2011.

Its comparative cheapness, easy availability, reliability, and impeccable flying characteristics have seen the CJ-6 become a widespread 'warbird', with several hundred civilian-owned examples airworthy worldwide. In its original role with the PLAAF, however, the CJ-6 has for some time been expected to be replaced by the Hongdu/Yakovlev CJ-7 primary trainer, though the exact status of that aircraft is somewhat unclear, having yet to enter service despite first flying in 2010.

Nanchang CJ-6
Weight (Maximum take-off): 1400kg (3086lb)
Dimensions: Length 8.46m (27ft 9in), Wingspan 10.22m (33ft 6in), Height 3.3m (10ft 10in)
Powerplant: One 213kW (286hp) Zhouzhou HS-6A (Ivchenko AI-14) nine cylinder, air-cooled radial piston engine
Maximum speed: 370km/h (230mph)
Range: 700km (430 miles)
Ceiling: 6250m (20,510ft)
Crew: 2
Armament: Usually none but provision for two 7.62mm (0.3in) machine guns fixed forward firing in nose

Nanchang CJ-6
A PLAAF CJ-6. This sturdy low-cost aircraft has been deployed by a variety of air forces, including Albania, Bangladesh, Cambodia, Laos, Sri Lanka and Zambia.

118

Hongdu JL-8

Produced in cooperation with the Pakistan Aeronautical Complex, the JL-8 entered service with the PLAAF in 1994. Over 300 have been built for Chinese forces, and the aircraft has proved an export success, operating with 15 other nations to date.

Hongdu JL-8
This JL-8 'No. 6' was seen at Changchun Dafangshen Airbase in July 2023.

Proposed as a joint venture in 1986, with design work beginning the following year, the first JL-8 prototype took to the skies for the first time in November 1990. A pre-production batch of 24 was evaluated in 1994; 18 in China, and the remaining six in Pakistan, where the aircraft is referred to as the Karakorum-8 or simply K-8. The PLAAF began to receive serial production aircraft in 1995, and the JL-8 has been in production ever since, with current fleet size believed to be 350 plus an additional 16 with the People's Liberation Army Naval Air Force.

Popular type

A conventional intermediate jet trainer, the JL-8 replaced several obsolete types in the Chinese inventory such as the Shenyang JJ-5, derived from the 1950s vintage MiG-17. Intended to be as cost-effective as possible, with a short turn-around time and low maintenance requirements, the type has proved attractive to less wealthy nations and has been the subject of major export orders. Eighty unassembled aircraft were delivered to Egypt (and designated K-8E) in 2005 for example, to be followed by local production of the type, and Venezuela have ordered 58.

Non-Chinese aircraft are usually fitted with the US Honeywell TFE731 engine rather than the WS-11 (a Chinese licence-built Ivchenko AI-25) of aircraft utilized in the PLAAF. As well as its primary training role, the JL-8/K-8 can easily be configured for airfield defence and light attack missions – in some air arms, this is its primary mission.

Bolivia took delivery of six JL-8VBs specifically for use in anti-drug operations, and K-8s of the Myanmar Air Force have been used in action to strike Kachin Independence Army positions in the north of the country.

Hongdu JL-8
Weight (Maximum take-off): 4330kg (9546lb)
Dimensions: Length 11.6m (38ft 1in), Wingspan 9.63m (31ft 7in), Height 4.1m (13ft 5in)
Powerplant: One 16.01kN (3600lbf) thrust Honeywell TFE731-2A turbofan engine
Maximum speed: 800km/h (500mph)
Range: 2250km (1400 miles)
Ceiling: 13,000m (43,000ft)
Crew: 2
Armament: Five hardpoints for a total of up to 1000kg (2205lb) external stores, including 23mm (0.9in) gun pod (centreline only), missiles, bombs or fuel tanks

TRAINERS

Guizhou JL-9

A remarkable example of incremental development, the JL-9 combines a 21st-century wing and glass cockpit with the mid-1950s rear fuselage and tail surfaces of the MiG-21, versions of which have been produced in China since 1964.

Revealed by Guizhou in 2001 at Zhuhai airshow, the FTC-2000 (Fighter Trainer China-2000) programme began as a private venture to deliver an inexpensive but effective training platform for fourth-generation fighter aircraft. The Chengdu JJ-7 trainer, a two-seat training version of the J-7 fighter (a Chinese-produced development of the MiG-21), was utilized as a basis for the new aircraft to minimize costs, and the engine, empennage and mechanical controls of the JJ-7 were retained.

Early development
The FTC-2000 featured a new double-delta wing, a forward fuselage with side air intakes, a nose containing a JL-10GJ X-band pulse-Doppler fire-control radar with a 30km (48 miles) range and a glass cockpit. A new stepped cockpit and canopy design gave both student and instructor much better forward and downward views than the JJ-7, and the crew benefitted from much improved avionics. The aircraft flew for the first time on 13 December 2003, and compared with the rival Hongdu JL-10, which flew slightly more than two years later, the FTC-2000 was considered technologically inferior but was cheaper and available more quickly. Both types have subsequently entered production and service in China.

First deliveries
The first batch of FTC-2000s was delivered to the PLAAF for evaluation in 2008, at which time the aircraft was designated JL-9 Mountain Eagle, FTC-2000 being retained as the export designation. After tests and certification, the aircraft began to enter regular PLAAF service in 2014. By 2023, a reported fleet of 30 was in service. Intended to replace the JJ-7

Guizhou JL-9
Weight (Maximum take-off): 9850kg (21,716lb)
Dimensions: Length 14.55m (47ft 9in), Wingspan 8.32m (27ft 4in), Height 4.1m (13ft 5in)
Powerplant: One 53.89 kN (12,110lbf) thrust dry (76.53 kN (17,200lbf) with afterburner) WP-14C Kunlun-3 turbojet engine
Maximum speed: (approx) 1480km/h (920mph)
Range: 2500km (1553 miles) with maximum external fuel
Ceiling: 16,000m (52,490ft)
Crew: 2
Armament: One 23mm (0.9in) machine gun fixed, forward firing in forward fuselage; five hardpoints for a total of up to 2000kg (4409lb) external stores, including missiles, bombs or fuel tanks

---

Guizhou JL-9
The JL-9 advanced jet trainer has been in service with the PLAAF since 2014.

as the trainer for pilots transitioning to the J-7 and J-8, the JL-9 is considered insufficient for the training of J-10 and J-11 crews, a role undertaken by the JL-10.

Swordfish

Later variants include a dedicated naval version for carrying out simulated carrier landings for training PLAN pilots. Known as the JL-9G Swordfish, it made its maiden flight in 2009. The first prototype was fitted with an arrestor hook. Unfortunately, the hook turned out to be causing too much stress to the airframe, and the aircraft was deemed unsuitable for arrested landings. Therefore, the JL-9G can only simulate take-off from the ski-jump and non-arrested landings under the guidance of LSO and OLS and entered service by late 2013. Guizhou has reportedly developed a version with a redesigned rear fuselage and tail hook installed.

This improved JL-9GA was first flown in 2020 and features wingtip decelerons to better simulate the low speed and high angle of attack approach required for carrier landings.

The FTC-2000's cheap price and ready availability have seen it achieve modest export success, with small numbers sold to both Myanmar and Sudan thus far.

The FTC-2000G multi-role fighter trainer was the type acquired by Myanmar, and at the time of delivery in late 2022, the type was considered the cheapest light fighter available anywhere in the world. This version is heavier and slower than the standard trainer – though still capable of Mach 1.2 – and possesses a different wing design. With seven hardpoints, it can carry 3000kg (6614lb) of stores.

FTC-2000G

The FTC-2000G is the dual seat light combat aircraft/lead-in fighter trainer of the JL-9 type. The aircraft also features a diverterless supersonic inlet.

TRAINERS

Hongdu JL-10

An advanced trainer and light combat aircraft, the JL-10 was developed with the assistance of Yakovlev OKB in Russia. Both subsonic and supersonic variants have been produced, and the type is expected to replace both the JL-8 and JL-9 in PLAAF service.

In contrast to its rival, the JL-9, the Hongdu JL-10 was a clean-sheet design intended to feature such elements as fly-by-wire and HOTAS control for the student and instructor. In 2000, the Yakovlev Design Bureau was contracted as a technical and scientific consultancy for the aircraft then known as the L-15, a designation it retains for export versions. Yakovlev's influence in the design is readily apparent as the aircraft bears a strong resemblance to the Yak-130, over 100 of which serve with Russian Aerospace Forces, and notably utilizes the same engines as the Russian aircraft.

Maiden flights

Flown for the first time on 13 March 2006, the L-15 is a twin-engine aircraft of generally conventional layout and appearance for a 21st-century training aircraft. The aircraft sports advanced features, such as a glass cockpit (compatible with night vision goggles), and, like the Yak-130, is equipped with distinctive leading-edge extensions (LERX) and a large vertical fin and rudder. Both features are designed to impart excellent control at high angles of attack and are useful for simulating aspects of the J-10 and J-11 flight envelope unattainable to other training aircraft in the PLAAF inventory. The first variant to appear was the L-15 subsonic advanced trainer, which was the first to enter PLAAF service as the JL-10. Production aircraft were first observed in full PLAAF service during 2016. The other line of development for Chinese service is the supersonic lead-in fighter trainer (LIFT) variant. This was announced in 2010 but took a considerable time to appear as an after-burning version of the Ivchenko-Progress AI-222-25F turbofan engines proved subject to slow progress.

Nonetheless, the first L-15 advanced fighter trainer made its maiden flight in December 2017, and this variant also features a stretched nose containing a small passive

Hongdu JL-10

This JL-10, serial number 2510, was seen at Changchun Dafangshen Airbase in October 2019.

Hongdu JL-10

Weight (Maximum take-off): 1600kg (25,574lb)
Dimensions: Length 2.4m (40ft 8in), Wingspan 9.4m (30ft 10in), Height 4.7m (15ft 5in)
Powerplant: Two 24.7kN (5553lbf) static thrust dry (41.2 kN (9,262.13lbf) with afterburner) Ivchenko-Progress AI-222K-25F turbofan engines
Maximum speed: 1730km/h (1074mph)
Range: 2600km (1600 miles) with maximum external fuel
Ceiling: 16,000m (52,000ft)
Crew: 2
Armament: Nine hardpoints for a total of up to 3000kg (6618lb) external stores including missiles, bombs or fuel tanks

electronically scanned array radar with a range of around 75km (47 miles). The PLAAF started utilizing the JL-10 for LIFT in 2019, and when compared to the somewhat less sophisticated JL-9, the JL-10 reportedly reduces conversion training time for the more recent PLAAF aircraft designs.

International customers

The L-15 design had always been developed with an eye to the export market, and Zambia became the first foreign operator of the type after it ordered six examples of the L-15Z in 2012. Delivered by the end of 2017, the L-15Z can carry the PL-5EII air-to-air missile, LS-6 GPS/INS bombs and a belly 23mm (0.9in) gun pod and be used as a light attack aircraft. The UAE also ordered the L-15 in early 2023. The potential of the L-15 as a light attack asset was subsequently developed further by Hongdu in the form of the L-15B, which was announced at the Zouhai airshow of 2016. The first prototype appeared in April of the following year.

Able to carry a total payload of 3500kg (7716lb) on nine hardpoints, the L-15B is capable of Mach 1.4 and boasts a shorter take-off and landing distance than its subsonic predecessor. In addition, a subsonic attack variant has been developed from the L-15B as the L-15AW, and in 2019, evidence emerged that Hongdu was developing an L-15AW version for PLAAF service. Further development has seen the emergence of a naval variant with strengthened twin-wheel nose gear, launch bar and tail hook. Believed to be designated JL-10J, this variant will serve aboard the new carrier *Fujian*.

Air show

A Hongdu JL-10 trainer jet performs during the 2022 China Aviation Industry Conference and Nanchang Air Show on 26 November 2022.

Index

References to photographs are in *italics*.

AA-10 Alamo A missile *22, 38–9, 42*
AA-10 Alamo B missile *36*
AA-11 Archer missile *22*, 36, *38–9, 42*, 43
AA-12 Adder missile 21, 36, 40, 43
Aérospatiale Dauphin 2 103
Aérospatiale/Eurocopter AS332/ EC225 Super Puma 98
    AS 332L 98
Aérospatiale Super Frelon 101
Airbus A319 57, 76
    A319-115 57
Airbus Helicopters H225 98
AKD-9 missile 105
AKD-10 missile *104*, 105
Algeria 110, 112
Antonov An-2 Colt 56
Antonov An-12 Cub 64
Antonov An-24 62
Antonov An-30 Clank 74–5
    An-30A 74
    An-30B 74
    An-30D 74
AR-1 missile *109*
AR-2 missile *109*, 115
AR-3 missile 115
AR-4 missile 115
AS-14 Kedge missile 40
AS-17 Krypton missiles 40, 53
AS-18 Kazoo 40

BA-7 missile 111, 112
BA-21 missile 104
Beijing University of Aeronautics and Astronautics (BUAA) 108
Boeing 737 76–7
    737-3Q8 76
    737-76D 76
    737-85N 76
    737-300 77
    737-800 77
Bolivia 119
Bombardier CRJ 58–9
    CL-600-2B19 Challenger 600 58, 59
    CL-600-2C10 Challenger 870 58–59
    CRJ200ER 58
    CRJ700 58
    CRJ700ER 58
BZK-005 Giant Eagle 108, 109–10
    BZK-005B 109
    BZK-005C 110
BZK-007 Sunshine 108–9

C-701/K missile 115
CH-1 Rainbow 110
CH-2 Rainbow 110
CH-3 Rainbow 110
CH-4 Rainbow 110
CH-5 Rainbow 109, 110
CH-AS-X-13 missile *48*, 49
Changhe Z-8 101–2
    Avicopter AC313 102
    Z-8A 101
    Z-8F 102
    Z-8G 102
    Z-8KA 101
    Z-8L 102
    Z-18A/Z-8G 102
    Z-18F 102
    Z-18J AEW 102
Changhe Z-10 104
    Z-10K 104
    Z-10ME 104
Chengdu Aircraft Corporation (CAC) 111, 113
Chengdu Aircraft Research & Design Institute (CADI) 111, 112, 113
Chengdu GJ-2 111
Chengdu J-7 10–12
    F-7MG 12
    F-7PG 12
    J-7E 12

J-7EB 12
J-7EH 12
J-7FS *11*
J-7G 12
J-7I (J-7A) 10–11
J-7II (J-7A) 11
J-7IIA 11
J-7IIH 11
J-7III (J-7C) 11–12
J-7IIIA (J-7D) 12
J-7L 12
Chengdu J-10 Vigorous Dragon/ Firebird 15–19
J-9VI (J-9B) 15–16
J-10A *15*, 16, *16*, 18, 19
J-10AH 16
J-10AS 16–17, 18
J-10ASH 17
J-10AY 19
J-10B 18, 19, 32
J-10C 18–19
J-10CY 19
J-10D 19
J-10SY 19
Chengdu J-20 Mighty Dragon/ Firefang *8–9*, 30–3
J-20A 30, 32, 33
J-20S 32–3
China Aerospace Science and Technology Corporation (CASC) 110
Chinese Academy of Engineering 12
Chinese People's Armed Police Force 102, 105
CM-502 missile 115
Cultural Revolution 12, 50, 62

East China Sea 41, 48, 61, 79, 93, 109
Egypt 11, 110, 111, 112, 119
Ethiopia 111, 112
Eurocopter AS565 Panther 103

France 98, 101, 103

INDEX

FT-7 bomb 114
FT-8D missile 114
FT-9 bomb 114
FT-10 bomb 114

GB1/TG500 bomb 18
GJ-1/WD-1K Wing Loong (Pterosaur) I *106–7*, 110–11
GJ-2 Wing Loong II 111, 112
Guizhou Aircraft Industry Corporation (GAIC) 108, 111, 112, 113
Guizhou JL-9 120–1
  FTC-2000 120–1
  FTC-2000G 121
  JJ-7 120
  JL-9G Swordfish 121
  JL-9GA 121

Harbin Y-12 69
  Y-12C 69
  Y-12D 69
  Y-12F 69
  Y-12II 69
  Y-12IV 69
Harbin Z-9 103
  Z-9B 103
  Z-9C 103
  Z-9EC 103
  Z-9W 103
  Z-9WA 103
  Z-19 103
Harbin Z-20 *96–7*, 105
  Z-20F 105
  Z-20J 105
  Z-20K SAR/transport helicopter 105
  Z-20W 105
Hong Kong 78
Hongdu JL-8 119
  JL-8VB 119
  K-8E 119
Hongdu JL-10 *116–17*, 122–3
  JL-10J 123
  L-15 122–3
  L-15AW 123
  L-15B 123

L-15Z 123
lead-in fighter trainer (LIFT) 122

Ilyushin Il-76 Candid 60–1
  Il-76MD *54–5*, 60–1
  Il-76TD 60, 61
Ilyushin Il-78 60, 61
India 39, 78, 85, 109, 112
Indonesia 111
Iraq 101, 110
Israel 15–16, 86, 101

J-6W 108
Japan 79, 88, 93, 94, 95, 109
JG-500 bomb 28

KAB-500Kr bomb 40
KAB-1500Kr bomb 40
Kazakhstan 111
KD-9 missile 104
KD-10 missile 104, 111
KD-20 missile 48, 49
KD-63 missile 47, 48, 49
KD-63H missile 47
KD-88 missile 28
Kh-29 missile 40
Kh-31A missile 40
Kh-31P missile 14, 40, 53
Kh-59ME missile 40
Kh-59MK missile 40
KJ-2000 60
Komsomolskon-Amur Aircraft Production Association (KNAAPO) 20, 37, 39, 42

Learjet Model 35 and Model 36 78
  35A 78
  36A 78
Libya 101, 102, 112
LS-6 GPS/INS bomb 123
LS-500 bomb 28
LS-500J bomb 18

MiG-21 10
Mil Mi-17 and Mi-171 99–100
  Mi-17V5 100
  Mi-171E 100
  Mi-171Sh 100

Morocco 112
Myanmar 110, 119, 121

Nanchang CJ-6 118
  CJ-6A 118
  Haiyan A 118
  Haiyan B 118
  Haiyan C 118
Nanchang Y-5 56
  drone version 56
  Y-5B-200 56
  Y-5U 56
naval aircraft
  bombers and attack aircraft 24, 47, 48, 50, 51, 53
  fighters and interceptors 12, 13, 16, 17, 24, 40
  helicopters 102, 103, 105
  special mission aircraft 81, 82, 84, 85, 89, 90, *91*, 92–3, 95
  trainers 119, 121, 123
  transports 58, *59, 62*, 62, 63
North Korea 113, 114, 118

Pace, Gen Peter *35*
Pakistan *66*, 83, 103, 104, 110, 111, 112, 119
Paracel Islands, Battle of the (1974) 50
Peace Pearl programme 13
People's Liberation Army Air Force (PLAAF)
  1st August Demonstration Team 19
  1st Regiment, 1st Fighter Division *25*
  3rd Brigade, Northern Command *28*
  4th Regiment, 2nd Air Division *20*
  5th Regiment, 2nd Air Division *17*
  5th Transportation and SAR Brigade, Western Theatre *100*
  6th Regiment, 2nd Air Division *36*, 43
  9th Air Brigade, Eastern Command 31
  9th Air Regiment, 3rd Air Division 40

INDEX

10th Air Regiment, 4th Division 67
12th Air Regiment, 4th Division 69, 71
13th Division 61
13th Transport Division 60
15th Airborne Army *101*
15th Airborne Corps 69
19th Regiment, 7th Division *22*
34th Transport Division 79
44th Air Regiment, 15th Fighter Division, *11*
54th Brigade *38–9*
54th Regiment, 18th Division *37*
76th Electric Warfare Regiment, 26th Special Mission Division 81, 88
89th Brigade, Northern Theatre Command *23*
98th Air Brigade, Eastern Command *26*
100th Air Regiment, 34th Transport Division 57, 58, 76
102nd Air Regiment 76, 78
106th Aerial Survey Regiment, 36th Bomber Division 74
108th Air Regiment, 36th Bomber Division *47*
126th Air Brigade, *51*
172nd Air Brigade *30*
176th Air Brigade *33*
Independent (Aerial Survey) Regiment 74
Transportation and Search and Rescue Brigade *102*
Xinjiang Army Aviation Brigade *100*
People's Liberation Army Navy (PLAN) *see* naval aircraft
Philippines 85, 114
PL-2B missile 12
PL-5B missile 12
PL-5EII missile 123
PL-8 missile 11, 12, 17, *25*, 53
PL-8B missile 24
PL-10 missile 17, 24, 25, *26*, 27, 31
PL-11 missile 14, 17
PL-12 missile 14, 17, 24, *25*, 41

PL-15 missile 17, *23*, 25, *26*, 27, *29*, 31
PL-17 missile 28

R-27 missile *22, 36, 38–9, 42*
R-73 missile *22, 36, 38–9, 42*, 43
R-77 missile 21, 36, 40, 43
Rosoboronexport arms export agency 60–1
Russia/Soviet Union
 bombers and attack aircraft 46, 51, 53
 fighters and interceptors 10, 14, 16, 20–1, 22, 26, 31, 34–43
 helicopters 99–100
 special mission aircraft 74–5, 79, 86
 transports 56, 60–1, 62, 64, 71
 trainers 122

Saudi Arabia 110, 111
Shaanxi KJ-200 Moth 80–2
 KJ-200A 80, 81, 82
 KJ-200B 82
 KJ-200H 82
 Y-8GX-5 80
 Y-8GX-12 82
 Y-8W 80
 Y-9LG 82
Shaanxi KJ-500 83–5
 KJ-500A *72–3*, 84
 KJ-500H 84, 85
 Y-8GX-10 83
 Y-9W 83
 ZDK-03 83
Shaanxi Y-8 64–6
 Y-8A 64
 Y-8C 64, 65
 Y-8E 65
 Y-8F-100 65
 Y-8F400 66
 Y-8H 65
Shaanxi Y-8 & Y-9 special mission versions 89–95
 Y-8CB 89–90
 Y-8DZ 90
 Y-8F600 67
 Y-8G 92

Y-8GX-1 89–90
Y-8GX-2 Mace 89, 90, 92
Y-8GX-3 Mouse 92
Y-8GX-4 *91*, 92
Y-8GX-6 67–8
Y-8GX-6 March 92–3
Y-8GX-7 92
Y-8GX-8 Mist 93
Y-8GX-9 93
Y-8GX-11 94
Y-8GX-12 94
Y-8GX-13 94–5
Y-8GX-14 95
Y-8GX-15 95
Y-8J Mask 89, 90–1
Y-8JB 90
Y-8JZ Mist 90, 93
Y-8T 92
Y-8XZ 92
Y-8Q 92–3
Y-9 Claw 67–9
Y-9G 94
Y-9LG 94
Y-9Q 95
Y-9T 95
Y-9XZ 93, 94
Y-9YL 93
Y-9Z 94–5
Shenyang J-6W 108
Shenyang J-8 (Finback) 12–14
 J-7 12
 J-8A 12
 J-8B 12–14
 J-8BH (J-8DH) 14
 J-8C 13
 J-8D 13, 14
 J-8DF 14
 J-8F *13*, 14
 J-8G 14
 J-8H 14
 J-8I (J-8A) 12
 J-8II Batch 02 13
 J-8II (J-8B) 12–13
 J-8IIA (J-8B) 13, 14
 J-8IIB 14
 J-8IIB (J-8D) 13, 14
 J-8III (J-8C) 13
 J-9 12

INDEX

JZ-8 14
JZ-8F *13*, 14
Shenyang J-11 and J-11A 20–2
  J-11B 21–2
Shenyang J-11B (Flanker-L) 21–2, 23–5
  J-11BG 24
  J-11BGH 24
  J-11BH 24
  J-11BS 24, *24*
  J-11BSH 24
Shenyang J-11D 25, 26
Shenyang J-16 7, 23, 26–9
  J-16D 29
Sichuan earthquake 101–2
Sichuan Lantian Helicopter Company 100
Sichuan Tengden Technology 114
Sikorsky UH-60 Blackhawk 105
South Africa 101
South China Sea 43, 48, 61, 62, 82, 85, 94, 109
Soviet Union *see* Russia/Soviet Union
Spratly Islands 85, 94, 109
Stockholm International Peace Research Institute (SIPRI) 78
Sudan 101, 121
Sukhoi Su-27 Flanker 14, 34–6
  Su-27M (T-10M) 41–2
  Su-27SK Flanker-B 20–1, 22, 34, *35*, 36
  Su-27UB 34
  Su-27UBK Flanker-C 20, 24, 34, 36
Sukhoi Su-30 Flanker-G 37–41
  Su-27PU 37
  Su-30MK 37, 39
  Su-30MK2 37, 40–1
  Su-30MKI 39
  Su-30MKK 37, 38–41, 51, 61
Sukhoi Su-35 Flanker-E 41–3
  Su-35BM 42
  Su-35S 42
Sukhoi T-10 34
  T-10S 34
Syria 101

Taiwan 43, 85, 88, 93, 94, 95, 109, 114
tankers 48, 61, 71
TB-001 Twin-Tailed Scorpion 114–15
  TB-001A 115
Tiananmen Square 13, 34, 99, 105, *108*
Tibet 65, 85, 109, 112, 114
Tupolev Tu-16 46
Tupolev Tu-154 Careless 79
  Tu-154M 79
  Tu-154M/D 79
TY-90 missile 104

UAE 111, 112, 123
Ukraine 61, 67, 69–70
United States 13, 30, *35*, 65, 66, 76, 86, 90, 99, 104, 105
Uzbekistan 60, 111

Venezuela 119
Vietnam 50, 78, 85

Wing Loong I 110–11
  Wing Loong 1D 112
  Wing Loong 1E 110
Wing Loong II 111, 112
Wing Loong 10 113
WZ-5 65–6
WZ-7 Soaring Dragon 113–14
WZ-9 Divine Eagle 115
WZ-10 Cloud Shadow 113
WZ-10 Wing Loong 10 (Wind Shadow 112–13

Xi'an H-6 Badger 46–9
  H-6A 46
  H-6D 46–7
  H-6DU 47, 48
  H-6E 46
  H-6F 46
  H-6G 47
  H-6H 47
  H-6J 48–9
  H-6K *44–5*, 46–7, 48, *49*, 79
  H-6L 47
  H-6M 47–8

  H-6N 48–9
  HU-6 48
Xi'an JH-7 Flounder/Flying Leopard 50–3
  H-7 50
  JH-7A 50–1, 51–3
Xi'an KJ-2000 Mainring 86–8
  A-50I 86, 88
  KJ-3000 87
Xi'an Y-7 62–3
  HYJ-7 63
  MA-60 62
  Y-7-100 62
  Y-7-100C2 63
  Y-7G 62–3
  Y-7H 62
  Y-7H-500 62
  Y-7LH 63
Xi'an Y-20 Kunpeng *6*, 69–71
  Y-20A 70, 71
  Y-20B 71
  YY-20 71
  YY-20A 71
  YY-20B 71

Yakovlev Design Bureau 122
YJ-6 missile 47
YJ-8 missiles 51
YJ-12 missile 47, 48
YJ-83 missile 52
YJ-83K missiles 28, 47
YJ-91 missile 14, 18, 28, 29, 52–3
YJ-91A missile 47
YZ-100 bomb 111

Zambia 123

Picture Credits

PHOTOGRAPHS

Alamy: 24 (Imaginechina), 38 (Xinhua), 52 (Stocktrek Images), 96 (Xinhua), 106 (Imaginechina), 121 (Zuma Press)

Dreamstime: 47 (Zjm7100), 81 (Henryike)

Getty Images: 11 (Thomas Klar), 14 (Goh Chai Hin/AFP), 21 (Future Publishing), 56, 66 & 88 (AFP), 108 (Asahi Shimbun), 109 (Power Sport Images), 112 (Bloomberg), 116 (Future Publishing)

Getty Images/Visual China Group: 7, 8, 27, 31, 68, 72, 84, 110, 111, 113, 114, 123

GNU Free Documentation Licence Version 1.2: 40 (Dimitriy Pichugin)

Licensed under the Creative Commons Attribution-Share alike 4.0 Licence: 33 (Alert5)

Ministry of National Defense of the Republic of China: 91

Shutterstock: 18 (plavi011), 22 (Dave Colman), 54 (Media_works), 76 (Konwicki Marcin), 102 (EarnestTse)

Shutterstock/Fasttailwind: 6, 15, 16, 43, 44, 49, 53, 70

U.S. Department of Defence: 35 (Staff Sgt D. Myles Cullen)

ARTWORKS

Edward Jackson (artbyedo): 64, 65, 80–85, 89–95, 105

Pavel Matviyenko: 99, 118–122

Rolando Ugolini: 10, 13, 46–51, 57–63, 74–79, 86/87, 98, 103

Teasel Studios: 5, 17–42, 67, 69, 100–102, 104